First Published in 1991 by:

**Armida Press
Post Office Box 1210
Kapaa, HI 96746**

ISBN: 0-9628396-3-9
Library of Congress Catalogue No: 90-85690

Printed in the United States of America

### Disclaimer

The information in this book is being written from personal experience. It is not being offered as a recommendation for anyone as a particular path of healing to follow. It is not the intention of the author to prescribe for any conditions, physical or otherwise. The manner in which this material is interpreted and used is the sole responsibility of the reader.

# ACKNOWLEDGEMENTS

I would like to utilize this space to recognize those individuals who have, in some way, given me the support and belief I needed to make this book possible. These individuals have been wonderful to me and given me so much. My words seem inadequate to truly express my gratitude. It is from individuals such as these mentioned that I receive the strength and conviction needed to share my experiences. Many times in my life, were it not for the undying and unconditional love that these individuals have given, I would have transcended the earth plane. My life has not been an easy one, but thanks to my wonderful friends, it has been a very full one. To all of you, I give you my sincere mahalo (thanks) and offer you my love and devotion eternally:

Don and Diane Burt (my parents), Jimmy Coleman, Gurudeva, Ceyon Swami, Sadhaka Haranandi, all of the Monks at The Church of San Marga, Serge King, Edward Long, Kristen Pugliese, Dena Walker, Deva Vani, Rama, Rose VanDreel, Dale True, Pasha Turley, Nancy and Hal Booth, Glenna Foster, Kathy Schlincover, Marlen and Mike McDowell, Raphael, Vanessa Simhauser, Kai Yutah Clouds, Belinda Chambers, Bob and Lavonne Rivera, Isani Pointus, Ruth Richmond, Vicki Andrews, Lehshel Wilkinson, my friends at the Mount Vernon Co-op, Stephen Weinberg, Robin Bolack, Christie Whitfield, Giving Love, Amithea Majesty Love, Zion Love, and My Beloved Husband Christopher A. Zion, whose support and love has definitely made this book possible.

*Special thanks to the following women:*

| | | |
|---|---|---|
| Alexandra Mines | ———— | Editing |
| Chris Stewart | ———— | Proofreading |
| Antoinette Park | ———— | Cover Layout |
| Tamzin Williams | ———— | Page Design & Typesetting |

My Aloha
**Almitra Sunrise Zion**

# Dedication

This book is dedicated to the manifestation of the
Iraivan Temple, home of the Earthkeeper crystal, located
at the San Marga Sanctuary on the Island of Kauai.
And it is dedicated to those sacred few whose feet on a
narrow path of truth walk in dedication to the
vision of peace and harmony whose lives I have been
blessed to touch via the wondrous mineral kingdom.
For each soul devoted to the wisdom and power of their
higher self (the universal spirit of God), I walk with
you. To these warriors of the light, seekers of the truth,
I am devoted.

In serving the light thee shall be served by the light.

All My Aloha, Eternally Yours,

Almitra Sunrise Zion

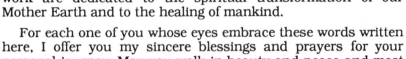

## Dearest Readers:

I offer you this book sincerely from my heart hoping that it will give you an understanding of the beauty and miracles awaiting you via the wonderous mineral kingdom. My life and work are dedicated to the spiritual transformation of our Mother Earth and to the healing of mankind.

For each one of you whose eyes embrace these words written here, I offer you my sincere blessings and prayers for your personal journey. May you walk in beauty and peace and most of all, in harmony with our Earth Mother.

Aloha, *Almitra Sunrise Zion*

# *Table of Contents:*

# INTRODUCTION

*I began working with crystals again about ten years ago.
I say again because I feel strongly that, on one's path, a
soul makes many journeys to this plane, and because of the
strong recall of information, I know for certain it's not
the first time my soul has worked with the mineral kingdom.*

*At the time, one could find very little information on
the uses of gems and crystals. It wasn't until many years to
follow that the books and teachers came forth to share
in the open about working with gems. For me, it has all come
firsthand from the stones, and from my personal
experience working with them. Since I began working with
the first crystal that came to me, I have been on an
incredible journey— A Crystal Journey. It is this journey I am
writing about, to share with you how I arrived at what
stones to use for what purposes and exactly what they can do
for us. I have a great deal of respect for channeled
information. While I'll admit that I'm very selective, I also feel
that one who has just been introduced to crystals and
gems has a hard time figuring out where this channeled
information should be placed. Is it fiction or non-fiction?
Has it really occurred, or what? Therefore, I offer this book as
a bridge to bring understanding among all the different
levels. I feel strongly that, because this information I am
sharing has already occurred on this level of reality, it
will help to open the doors of acceptance for the work we are
doing with the mineral kingdom and the truth it has to
offer us. I can appreciate how it could be hard for a beginner
to understand a lot of what is available by way of*

channeled information when the individual who has written the book has no real personal experience working with the stones. I feel that we are in a very crucial time where people want to know what the truth really is, and with all of the different movements cropping up today, there comes a lot of confusion. I'm offering this book to bring clarity. I know that by sharing my personal experiences as they have unfolded on my journey, it will help people to recognize that, indeed, there is something real to all of this. It is through our personal experiences that we become aware of what works and what doesn't. Because I have seen so much over the past ten years, I know for certain that the mineral kingdom has a great wealth of help for us on all levels. I share with you these experiences sincerely and with dedication to the mineral kingdom. The rocks have given me much over the years and have become my very dear friends. I use rocks in every aspect of my life. I have incorporated them into my healing work and use them on a daily basis to help me. I have spent hours teaching and sharing with others about them, and will continue to do so. I know for certain that the rocks and their part in my life is much deeper than a current fad or something that I will grow tired of.

When I began this work ten years ago, it was very different than it is today. Individuals who were not afraid to share the truth about the gems, or to say that rocks talk, or that a crystal could give you more energy, had to be willing to get laughed at. A few of us who were brave enough kept talking as others kept laughing. Today, through the devotion of this small group of souls, we see things opening up. This brings me a lot of joy personally. It's so wonderful to be able to work with people who have an open mind and who do not come to me only as a last resort.

*I have seen so much change in the last five years on this level. People want the information, and they are interested. Instead of laughing, they now listen and ask me to share more. This is exciting. I see my work expanding as the fear lets go. I work with all different kinds of people from all different ages and walks of life.*

*I see myself as a pioneer, not afraid to try something new (much like Columbus, who went around shouting that the world wasn't flat). When I first began doing healing massage, I got all kinds of responses from people. Very often I heard the response, "Oh, you touch people's bodies!" Slowly and gently, we go forward. Now massage is very accepted. I had the same experience in the beginning stages of my work with crystals and other gems. People thought I was nuts! I figured that was okay, and I felt comfortable in sharing the truth about my experiences. Well, ten years go by, and as one shares the truth about their experiences, slowly the walls come down. This book is another step in tearing down the walls. It is written to share the truth and experiences that testify to the reality of the crystal work and to share the true gift that the mineral kingdom is for us. I offer this sincerely, in hopes that you may better understand the mineral kingdom, and that you can incorporate these wondrous tools into your life. I know for certain that we could reach our goals without their help, but I view the situation in much the same light as I do this computer I'm writing on. Surely I could accomplish my goal without the computer. I could write everything out, or I could use a manual typewriter. But what a difference it makes for my work! The same holds true for the crystals I use in my work. Surely I could do it without them, but what a difference they make. If I can improve my results a hundred times over, would I not choose the tools that* will assist me?  Well, the minerals and gems are here to assist. They have come out in a time when mankind needs great help, so why not use whatever we can to make the job easier and better?  To put it simply, if it works, use it. The truth lies in the results. If it doesn't work, throw it out and use something else. For me the gems work, and that is why I use them.  I'm a person who bases a lot on results.  Over and over again I have witnessed amazing results when I work with the stones. Thank you for choosing this book, and know, too, that the  proceeds will be used to help further the work of the gem and mineral kingdom, for I have pledged one-half of all profits to the general building fund for the Iraivan Temple now in the process of being built on Kauai. This temple is being built for the people of the world, and will house the large crystal that came to me in a vision. The story of this vision and my journey to find the crystal are shared in Chapter Two (The Journey Home). This book is written directly from my personal experiences and is my own true story. I offer it sincerely to you as my personal testimony concerning the work of the gem and mineral kingdom.

— Almitra Sunrise Zion

Chapter One

# **Clarity**

The ability to accept a person just where they are at
gives one incredible peace.

*I would like to take this opportunity to share my truth as it
has unfolded in my life. I would like to express my respect for
each person's own unique spiritual path. I see all paths
leading us to the same end--to one God united in Love. I honor
each Master who has come to the earth to represent the light
of God.*

*It is not my place to offer or suggest any particular path to
anyone. I strongly feel that only each person, alone, can find
this for themselves. Therefore, I will continue to live my life
and dedicate my work to the supreme God, one united in love
and truth for all of mankind.*

*I do not consider myself to be a person who falls under the
title of "New Ager". Instead, I follow the path of the Ancient
Age. Everything I currently use in my life as a tool for my
divine work represents ancient information; knowledge that
has resurfaced only at this time.*

*I know that crystals and the understanding of the mineral
kingdom are a part of my eternal soul—my never-ending
oneness with God.*

*My life was devoted to the service of God at an early age.
I have walked a narrow path in unison with this divine
guidance, always offering all I do to this supreme Master.*

I honor and love Christ and offer my service always to represent the light of God. I respect all paths and see them as each soul's divine order to unfold their own personal path.

My path has unfolded slowly over many years. I have been working with crystals for over ten years now, and the path unfolded in line with my sincere love and devotion to the Christ Light. Therefore, I will continue to represent this light in the healing and teaching work that I do. I strongly believe in the creation of God and know that, surely, there was a divine plan intended for the mineral kingdom when God created each rock, each crystal and each gem.

All power comes only from God, and our tools are a service for this power. If one sets a crystal on a shelf, it is indeed a rock. Once one chooses to pick up this rock, it becomes a tool that can be used for good or bad. Therefore, I will challenge the statements being made that crystals and rocks are evil or dark energy. The crystals were misused in the past. This time around, they refuse to be misused, or to be in the hands of the wrong energies. I have seen this fact demonstrated--where individuals were using the crystals for the wrong purpose, and where greed and power were being misused. I have witnessed the crystals completely leaving the hands of such individuals.

I challenge each person to examine statements from within their own being. Don't let someone else's fear or unclarity be your final judgment; likewise, one should challenge blanket statements being made by certain religious leaders who claim crystals are dark energy. Question their sources. Have these individuals had any personal experiences with crystals, or are they simply passing on a statement that they have, in turn, agreed to represent? Time and time again, I have seen certain religious leaders instilling fear in people when they actually have no real foundation or reason for promoting that fear. Seek the divine guidance that is available to each of you. Call upon God to reveal the answers directly to you, and make your own decision based on what feels right to you.

I began healing work in the form of hands-on healing at the age of twelve. My path since then has become clearer, more devoted, and my healing work only better. I have devoted my life to the divine light of Christ, God, Love. I have walked a very narrow path relying on my direct connection with God. Others are often quick to judge based on their own lack of understanding. My brothers and sisters in Christ have attacked and accused me of actions I wouldn't dream of, simply because I work with crystals and herbs for healing. I offer classes to help others understand the wonderous gifts of the mineral kingdom, and do so to share how we can better understand and cooperate with God's creation. I do not hold anything but love for all of you. I bless you all, and will continue to thank you. My strength grows and my path is crystal clear.

I will continue to walk on the path God has put before me. I beckon each of you to do the same. Let us lay down our judgments and pick up the Cross of Truth. Let us follow in the true footsteps of Christ, offering our unconditional love to each person, regardless of whether or not they are walking the same path as ours. After living in Hawaii for over twelve years, I have been blessed to experience many spiritual paths. I have taken it upon myself to study and to better understand many different spiritual ways — the Hindu, Buddhist, Catholic, Protestant, Methodist, Krishna, Born Again Christian, Mormon, and Hawaiian Huna religions. I respect

3

*each individual's path, and support their right to express their beliefs. I will continue to walk on the path as a universal minister devoted to the unification of all paths united in unconditional love. I pray that in sharing my personal experiences, one will begin to see that crystals and rocks are truly a gift from God. In the hands of a person who chooses to use them for the good, they can truly support God's work.*

Chapter Two

# The Journey Home

How does one go about finding something they have only seen in
their mind, not knowing if or where, in fact, it exists?

*The large crystal first appeared to me in a vision while I
was living on Kauai. The vision was very clear and contained
a lot of details that helped me to understand the importance of
the mission I had been given. The vision was a very strong
one, and it continued to appear to me over a two-year period.
Finally, it was obvious that I had to complete the vision and go
in search of the crystal that, for some reason, had called upon
me to find it.*

*I tend to be the kind of person who holds a great deal of
dedication for something that is given to me from a vision or a
request from higher guidance. After receiving this vision and
the amount of energy that seemed to follow it over a two-year
period, I became very compelled to find the crystal and
complete the task. I would like to share the vision with you in
detail, and how it first appeared to me in my third eye. I will
do my best to bring you into the moment of when it first
arrived. Its clarity and detail were incredible. I have been
given visions all my life. As far back as I can remember, I have
been able to see things on another level. It has taken me years
to understand this level, and only just recently have I felt that
the world is ready to receive and understand people like
myself, and the gift of visions.*

*One needs to understand that visions are very different than dreams. Visions occur in one's mind (third eye). They occur while the person is awake. Often, the person will be in a state of meditation or relaxation, but not always. A vision is different than a thought or an attempt to imagine something. It is much like daydreaming and seeing yourself somewhere else. Basically, the visions I have come very unexpectedly. I am not in any particular frame of mind, and I don't set out consciously to have them. They usually occur in the daytime and start with a flash of light. I'm sometimes taken by surprise because they come very quickly. The vision of the large crystal came to me in this way. All of a sudden, a large crystal appeared in my third eye. It was immense to me since, up to this point, I had not ever seen or heard of a crystal of that size. The crystal was out-of-doors, and the details of the area were very specific. I was given the impression that the place in the vision was of a high altitude, since it was not close to the water. There was a definite vortex-energy present. The light around the crystal was illuminating. There was an obvious circle pattern to the area around the crystal, and in the distance, I could see mountains in the background. Standing before me in the vision was this incredible crystal. It stood before me almost parallel to my hips. The details of its formation were mind-blowing. The sides were smooth, and they converged to form a perfect point at the top of the crystal. It was slender at the base-approximately two feet-and rose to a six-pointed formation at the top. The perfection of the pointed top was very imprinted upon my mind. This detail was so clear that I knew this crystal was very special. The energy coming through it was very focused. The crystal was perfectly white in color and had a very obvious green light (aura) emanating from it.*

*This vision occurred to me two years before I was able to go and find the crystal. The vision I described to you was as it first appeared to me. I had several recurring visions of this crystal over the next two-year period, and it was always the same. It would stand before me in my mind and beam at me. I became very familiar with the crystal over the two-year period. I became very close to it, feeling that we were old friends. One time there was a difference in the vision, however. The crystal was standing in the middle of a circle of twenty-one people. The crystal looked the same (it always appeared exactly the same-the size and the detail never changed). The people standing around the crystal had their right hands stretched out toward the crystal and their left hands with the palms up at their sides, level with their chests. They were standing with their eyes closed, and someone was guiding them in an exercise of programming the crystal for world peace. It was understood that no one was to touch the crystal. It was mounted in the center of a structure, and people were coming there to experience the energy. All of the people were very peaceful and quiet. Again, I could see the mountains in the background and the circle of energy around the area on the ground, and I got a distinct feeling that the ocean was far away. This particular vision of the crystal had a strong impact on me. It became very clear that there was something trying to come through to me from this crystal. I felt a strong need to find the crystal and get it to Kauai. At this point, I felt that I had been given a mission to find this stone and to get it to the right place. I knew that there was going to be a temple built, and it was obvious that the crystal was going to make its home there. The clarity of this particular vision allowed me to receive the full impact of the message.*

Once I saw the crystal being programmed for peace, and saw the people coming, I knew there had to be a very special place for it. It was at this juncture that I completely took the vision into my heart. I vowed to the Universe that I would indeed do my best to find the crystal and get it to Kauai.

At the time I had the original vision and then its variation, I wasn't aware of anyone attempting to build a temple. I was studying with Serge King, who is a Kahuna master. He was working with a group of people to buy land in Kilauea, and to build a spiritual center that would teach the way of Aloha through the ancient Huna teachings. I was taken to the land that he was attempting to acquire. I thought that perhaps this was where the crystal was supposed to go. But when I went there, I realized it was not the place in my vision. The ocean was too close by, and the obvious circle pattern on the ground was not present. Also, I could not see the mountains in the distance. I knew nothing of Gurudeva and the temple that was in Wailua, or his vison of the crystal temple that he was dedicated to building. I only knew that I had to go find this crystal or I would never have any peace, as it would not leave me alone. Therefore, at the end of two years, things had really accellerated. I was now fully involved in working with crystals. I had been working with the mineral kindgom for about four years at that time. I had been active in working with the stones for healing, and was teaching workshops about crystals, their properties, and how to use them. I had just recently expanded my business, opening a store on the Island. The store was devoted entirely to crystals and minerals. We also carried a small selection of New Age books. I really enjoyed having a place where people could come and experience the crystals. It was amazing to see how the people would arrive and spend hours there. We would share knowledge about the stones, and people would just enjoy their energy. It was particulary fun for me to work with people who thought that the whole thing about crystals was just a bunch of nonsense. I would work with these individuals and give them a few demonstrations so that, beyond anything else, they could see for themselves how the crystals worked. Our timing was perfect. The month following the opening of the store, Shirley Maclaine's movie and books were reaching the general public, and the whole crystal vibration was reawakening for modern America. I laughed to myself at the skepticism of folks around us when we decided to open a store specializing in crystals. I was really sincere in wanting to devote a store to the crystals-to be able to create a really nice atmosphere, and to create a vibration that was clear and conscious. In my heart, the mineral kinkgom was a way of life. The rocks had been a part of me for a long time. I wanted to share this with people on a level they could respect, given with sincerity and honesty. I felt that the crystals deserved to be presented in the right fashion. Therefore, we did our best to create a very lovely and professional atmosphere so that people could feel comfortable, especially if it was their first introduction to crystals. To me our store was a temple, a sacred place, and I always treated it that way.

One day while working at the store, I recieved a call from a monk at the temple. His name was Ceyon Swami. He called to let me know in advance that he and a few other swamis, along with Subumuneria (Gurudeva), would be coming to the store in a few hours. I said, "Sure, come on down!" I knew nothing of him or what a swami was, etc. Gurudeva is a Hindu guru and is involved with crystals by way of his path

in Hinduism. Hindus use crystals in their temples, and have
since the beginning of their religion (which is the oldest
religion known to man). This fact alone shows us that crystals
are, indeed, a part of our past, and not just a New Age
phenomenon or, as some folks insist, a passing fad.

Anyway, a few hours later, a van arrived in front of the
store and parked on the grass. The door opened and a group
of monks, all dressed the same with their hair pulled back,
came into the store. Ceyon Swami introduced himself to me.
I was in the room towards the middle of the store when
Gurudeva walked up to the counter where I was standing. His
presence had a very powerful effect on me. My body began to
vibrate all over, and I felt for a moment that I was going to fall
flat on my face. I could see a lot of energy around him, but
beyond that I felt as if I were standing before a long, lost
friend. He felt so familiar to me, that I knew he was an old
soul-friend. I kept looking at him, and at one point apologized
for staring at him so intensely. I told him that he reminded me
of someone very dear to me, and let it go at that. Then,
something very odd happened. All of a sudden, without
realizing why or even thinking about it, I began telling him
about my vision of the large crystal and how I was wanting to
find it and bring it to Kauai. He simply gave me a look that
went into my being. He said he believed that if the government
could afford to spend so much on warfare, that for the price of
one warhead, we could definitely buy the crystal. I was
amazed that I had even told him about my vision. Up until
that point, I had shared the vision only with my husband,
Christopher, and one friend that mined crystals. At the time,
I felt strange talking to him about it, and I had to question
myself as to why I had. Little did I know at the time that I was

a piece of a puzzle, and that Gurudeva had been having the same vision of the temple for two years. He had been actively searching for a large crystal for the focal point of the spadika (quartz crystal) Siva Lingam for the temple he was dedicated to building. As I have said before, the energy was accelerating, and the desire to complete the vision had become a passion with me. I had begun to feel as if someone had lit a fire underneath my rear to go find this crystal. Gurudeva had a great time in the store that day and spent a long time there with me . He complimented us on the job that we had done with our creation of the store and said that we had indeed created a beautiful temple. I spoke with him a little about my daughter, whom I had been actively seeking a teacher for. He invited me to bring her up to the temple to meet him. We arranged a time, and he instructed me on how to find the temple. A few days later, my daughter, Amithea, and I went up to the temple. It amazed me that in all the years I had lived on the same island as Gurudeva, I knew nothing of the temple or him. I was later told that the temple was a monastery and hadn't been open to the public. I really didn't know anything about the temple or the Hindu religion. I wanted to bring my daughter to meet with Gurudeva, as I was interested in helping her connect with a spiritual Master. I believe that each person coming to the earth has a different path or reason, and my daughter's path was definitely shown to my husband and I to stem from the east. The way she was born and the information that was given to us confirmed this fact over and over again. At that time she was five years old, and we had been searching for her teacher since the day she was born. In my mind, I was content in believing that the reason I had met with Gurudeva was to fulfill my daughter's need for a teacher.

11

*Little did I know that my involvement with this man would
include finding and bringing the crystal to him and the temple.
I was only interested in helping my daughter, who has an
obvious darma connection to the East Indian path. I wanted to
help her be able to receive what she needed. So, at the time,
I was going to see him simply to bring my daughter there. I
didn't give any thought to the large crystal and, quite
honestly, didn't get the connecton until much later as far as
the crystal was concerned. I was truly puzzled about why I
had shared the vision with him at all, and for a long time I
questioned myself about it. It seemed as though someone had
just taken control of my tongue, and had begun telling this
stranger (who really didn't feel like a stranger at all) about
the vision and my desire to bring the crystal home.*

*My visit to the temple was really fantastic. We met with
Gurudeva and he talked with my daughter as if he had
known her all her life. He had an immediate understanding
of who she was. I asked him a question that I had wanted an
answer to for a long time. I wanted to know why, if she was
an Indian soul, she had chosen to come to America instead of
going back to India. He told me that the best of India was
reincarnating in America, which made perfect sense to me
when I thought about it. Well, that day was the beginning of
a long friendship. We were able to establish a teacher for
Amithea, and one thing led to another.*

*It was a short time later when I heard from Ceyon Swami.
He contacted me in regard to my crystal classes, and asked if
I would give a class to the swamis and Gurudeva. I said that
I would be most happy to do so, and we made arrangements
for me to meet with them at the temple. They were interested
in learning more of the practical uses for crystals. They were*

very aware of crystals and had been actively using them in their temple worship, but had not been using them outside of the temple. I went to the temple and sat at a very long table, with myself at one end and the swamis seated around the table with Gurudeva at the other end. There were about twenty swamis at the class. I went through my regular presentation which lasts about three hours. Towards the end of the class, more and more crystals appeared. We talked about the different kinds of crystals, their uses and properties, and how to clear, charge, and program crystals. We covered a lot of information. I added a bit of humor to the presentation, as I found it very interesting to be seated among all of these swamis and teaching a class. Without being able to get some laughter going, I would have had a hard time. But I found them really interested in what I was saying. They were very polite and very wonderful to work with. It was one of the only times I have had a large group of men in one of my workshops. Most of the time, the women far outnumber the men.

From here, my connection with the temple kept growing, and I felt very connected with its energy and its people. I became close friends with Ceyon Swami. He was my main connection with the temple. When there was a need to talk or to get together, it was Ceyon I usually talked to. It was later on in the summer when Ceyon called me to arrange a class for the Hindu students who were coming to summer camp. The camp was for Hindu students from the mainland and outer Islands. I agreed to teach a class for the children and to spend the day working with them. Things accelerated, and we decided to combine the class with a visit to some of the vortex centers and power spots on Kauai. We decided to bring along

13

*a man who would put the class on video for later use in teaching about crystals. I arrived at the temple and gave a workshop (that lasted for the entire day) to about seventeen people, the majority being children. It was wonderful, because the level of understanding with the group of children was very evolved. They had remarkable knowledge about past lives, auras, chakras, and a lot of things that people usually don't know about in my workshops. Consequently, the information that came through was on a more advanced level than I can usually share. During the question period, I was asked about my vision of the large crystal, and what it looked like. By now the information had been shared openly with everyone at the temple, and it was understood that, somehow, I was going to locate this crystal. I received a lot of support in sharing my vision with this group of children, as they were aware of visions, and, being raised on a spiritual path, believed in the supernatural. At this point, it undoubtedly felt supernatural to me to go looking for a rock that had appeared in my mind, with no further detail as to where it was to be found.*

*By now my relationship with Ceyon Swami had grown. I felt comfortable in sharing with him. I realized that our relationship might be quite awkward at first because I was a female, and a swami usually has very little contact with the outside world. However, Ceyon felt like a very old friend. We ended up spending a lot of time together. One day, after we had spent the afternoon working to clear and charge some large generator crystals I had acquired for the temple, Ceyon gave me a ride home. We always had very deep conversations. I found him to be very refreshing from the average male because we could talk about things I dare not* talk about with most people. We could talk about cosmic things, the relationship with the earth, and the usual things that were part of my life and his. He had a great deal of information about astrology and past lives, and our belief systems were in harmony with one another. Ceyon gave me a ride home after we had a particularly long day together getting the crystals. He made a comment about how unusual it was for him to spend time with someone as extraordinary as myself. I asked him to explain further what he meant. He said that he very rarely spent time with others outside the temple, and that he found me very interesting. So with that, I went home.

My first experience with San Marga was quite wonderful. Again I spent the afternoon with Ceyon, as Gurudeva suggested that I go to San Marga and experience the energy there. San Marga is the physical place where the Iraivan temple is going to be built. Gurudeva told me that I would find the opening there, and to have a good time. When he said opening, I understood exactly what he meant. He was talking about an opening in the energy field-a doorway to the higher realms. I feel that the experience at San Marga that day really gave me the energy I needed to make the decision to go find the crystal. I had been given a very clear picture from the vision of the crystal as to the area it was to go. So when Ceyon took me there, it was very powerful for me in the way of connecting the vision with this level of here and now. It gave me a very poignant insight and understanding of the vision I had been given. The path to San Marga goes through a forest of rudraksha trees that were planted by the monks. The trees only grow in one other place in the world. Purple balls grow on them, and at the time they were all over the

**Gate to San Marga**

**Path to San Marga through Rudraksha Forest**

**Rudraksha Forest**

Path to San Marga

**On the path to Iraivan!**

On the path to Iraivan

On the path to Iraivan

Entrance to San Marga

ground. I was fascinated by the purple color, and I very
carefully selected three balls and held them in my hand.
Then, I continued the walk further down the path. It followed
a very straight line down through a field, and I got a very
strong sense of different energy levels as I continued forward.
Once I got near the end of the path, I felt a marked lift in the
energy as though I had passed through an energy vortex. At
the end of the path there were two very humble structures,
one on each side of the entrance. Inside the structures were
statues of the Hindu gods and a bell. Ceyon rang the bell,
and then we proceeded to the center of the field. It was when
I was walking towards the center of the field that I passed
through the opening that Gurudeva had talked about. It was
so incredible and obvious to me. The energy was moving in a
definite spiral up to the Universe, and I knew that it was a
doorway — a place where the worlds connected. It was
directly in front of this doorway that three large black rocks
were lying together on the ground. I was asking the Universe
for a sign, as I wanted to be shown for certain if this was the
place I had seen in my vision, and for certain if it was where
the crystal was to come home to. I sat down on the ground
before the three rocks and I began to focus on them. I felt a
strong energy coming from the rock on my right side and I put
my ear on it to listen to what it had to say. I had learned from
my American Indian teachers a long time ago that rocks will
talk if you will simply listen. I placed my ear to the rock and it
said ever so surely, "God himself dwells here." I was taken
aback at the message, and I sort of gasped as I sat up. I
looked directly at Ceyon and told him exactly what I had
heard. He took a breath, looked at me, and said, "That's
exactly what Gurudeva told me the rocks said!" I was still

**Sacred Rocks at San Marga Sanctuary**

*involved in getting a clear message from the earth, and was very involved in working with the area and being alert for any signs. For me, the owls are an omen and have always been a very special friend and Amakua (totem). I felt that there was an owl present in the area, and I began to focus on the energy as I sat on the ground before the rocks. I could feel the owl nearby, and as I stood up, turned around, and began walking, at that moment a very large white owl flew right in front of my face. I continued walking in a circle around the outer area of the rocks, and it was shown to me that there was a definite circle pattern to the area. I continued walking around the area, and as I walked, more and more was shown to me. First, the elements began to speak. It began to rain, and it continued to rain until I was very wet. Then the rain left and the sun came out, and in the distance I could see the mountains. This stood out in my mind, and I felt a very strong connection with the earth and the energy on this sacred place. It wasn't until much later that I was shown the drawing of the temple that Gurudeva was going to build on the grounds.*

*I left San Marga that day knowing for certain within the center of my being that this was indeed the place I had seen in my vision-the home for the crystal that at this time still existed only in my mind.*

*The events that followed were instrumental in leading me to the crystal. I never stopped to evaluate the situation. Now that I look back on it all, I guess it was a good idea that I hadn't. If I had ever really thought about the practical side of the task I was given, I would have dismissed the whole thing as impossible and left it at that. But for some reason, it never dawned on me that it was a difficult task. Instead, I was engrossed in the events that kept happening and the*

*overwhelming messages that kept coming to lead me
onwards. I tend to be the kind of person who goes with the
flow, and at the same time, I am very spontaneous. I will
move on an impulse or a strong feeling and credit my success
to the strong connection I maintain with my higher self (the
little voice within). Up until this point, I had no idea where to
begin to look for the crystal, and I had been told that they only
existed in Brazil and other countries. I examined this closely
with my inner self and felt no calling to leave the country, so
I disregarded that information. I was involved with a friend
from California at this time who I had met on Kauai. He was
a scientist and had been working with crystals. He had a
contact in Arkansas that he dealt with, and after our
connection on Kauai, I had asked him to send me some larger
crystals for the store. I had been wanting to offer people an
opportunity to have access to larger pieces, as up until this
point I had little available larger than a hand-held crystal.
My friend sent me a selection of larger clear quartz crystals
ranging from four pounds up to fifteen pounds. I was at the
store the day the crystals arrived. I was by myself working
and things were very busy that day. When I could, I went to
the back room and began to unwrap the crystals, carefully
placing them in the showcases. It was right after I opened the
box that the energy began to accelerate in the building. Above
the register in the front room was hanging a large glass mirror
with stained glass around it. I heard a loud crash as I was
unpacking the crystals. I walked into the front room, and there
lay the mirror unbroken on the floor. This amazed me, and I
watched very carefully as the energy continued to change the
more I unpacked the crystals. I normally would have taken
more time to look over the crystals as I unpacked them, but*

**Crystal that guided me to Arkansas**

*this time, because I was busy, I simply unpacked them,*
*cleared them with sagesmoke, and placed them out for*
*display. Once I had completed unpacking all the crystals,*
*I went about helping the customers in the store. Everyone was*
*completely amazed at the energy the new crystals had*
*brought and, of course, were excited to check them all out. I*
*was making my way to the other side of the room, and as I*
*passed by the counter where one of the new crystals was*
*sittting, I stopped in my steps as I heard a very obvious*
*command from this crystal to pick it up now. I was startled by*
*this, and as I opened the case, it slid out toward me. I picked*
*the crystal up and brought it directly up to my face, where I*
*examined it. The first thing that stood out in my mind was*
*that the face of the crystal was completely covered with very*
*small, raised pyramids. It was the first record keeper crystal I*
*had seen that was so obvious. The others I had seen so far*
*had only a few pyramids on the faces, and one had to look*
*hard to see them. On this crystal, however, the pyramids were*
*very apparent, and stood out clearly for one to see. I walked*
*to the office with the crystal and set it on my desk, because I*
*had just received a very clear message that this stone had*
*something it desperately wanted to tell me. I finished my day*
*at the store and headed home. I took the crystal with me, and*
*it has been with me ever since. I later learned that it came*
*from the mine I had visited during my journey to Arkansas.*
*That evening, I found a strong connection with my new crystal*
*friend. The crystal seemed alive and very anxious to share*
*some information with me. As I lay down for the evening, the*
*crystal found its way there with me.*
*Once one realizes that the earth is a living, breathing entity*
*that needs compassion and healing, they can begin their line*

*of service to assist her.*

*As I lay there with this fairly large crystal on my heart chakra, held carefully with both hands, I began to get very clear messages. The first thing it told me was the story of the journey it had made to find me, and the many different hands it had passed through to meet mine. I got this information in the form of gentle impressions flowing through my mind as I lay there holding the crystal and listening very carefully. When I heard the story of the search for our connection, it gave me a very compassionate, very sensitive feeling. Listening still, I received a very clear calling to go to Arkansas. I was given a very clear message that there were three reasons for me to go there, and how I could accomplish them. The first reason was to find the large crystal, the second involved selecting crystals to bring home for distribution, but the third was very vague. It came as a request from the earth herself for a healing and balancing. I was simply told that there was an imbalance in some part of the mining operation, and that I would be guided to where and how I could help. Needless to say, the crystal remained with me for the rest of the night. To this day, this particular crystal has been very instrumental in my life, and often spends the night on the end of my bed. I am always amazed at the difference in my dreams (and the messages I receive) when it is with me during sleep.*

*From this time forth, things really began to move. It became more and more obvious that it was time for me to, indeed, go and find the crystal. By that time, I at least knew where I was to go and, of course, that was a big plus. But still there remained the reality of how I was going to get there, etc. I can't remember exactly what happened next. I do remember*

*talking with my friend, Fred Bell, and he agreed to go with
me to Arkansas if I would work with him on acquiring some
crystals. He had one connection there whom he had been
purchasing crystals from. We agreed on a date to meet in
California, from where we would travel to Arkansas to meet
with the friend who would help me locate the crystals I
wanted. This was the beginning, and it took care of at least
part of the reasons I needed to go. Things truly flowed
together for the trip. I am always amazed at how things work
when one is in line with their purpose. Quite honestly, I made
the reservation for the trip without having the money to cover
it, and lacking any ideas about how I was going to pull it off.
I have learned through experience that, once one gets an idea,
puts out the energy, and moves ahead as if it is already
happening, all will come. Once again, I stepped forth on faith
that the money would come, made the flight arrangements,
and agreed to pay for the tickets the following week. Sure
enough, the next week I had all that I needed, and I was
amazed at the support the Universe was giving me.*

*Not only did I receive all the money that I needed, but my
dear friend, Kristin, who I had met the previous winter on
Kauai, agreed to meet me at the airport in California, and to
take me several hours by car right where I needed to go. She
also offered to help me with the rest of the funds I needed in
order to make a crystal purchase as per agreement with my
friend, Fred. It seemed that things were all set, and at last I
was going off to find the crystal, and to complete the vision
that had been given to me two years earlier. I had the
reservations and a plan of action, and I was getting ready on
a physical level. Now all I needed was the spiritual support
and energy that were required to complete this overwhelming
task.*

**Puja Ceremony**

*It was at this time when Ceyon Swami called me with an invitation to join him and Gurudeva for a Puja on the following Sunday morning. I was scheduled to leave on the following Monday morning to fly to Oahu, then to California, and then on to Arkansas. The following events truly gave me the support I needed on a higher level to follow through with the calling and complete my work. I met with Ceyon Swami for the Puja, which is an ancient Hindu ceremony whose purpose is to invoke the devas from the spiritual side, and to help one with their needs. I had never attended such a ceremony, but it felt all so familiar to me. I was given complete support from Gurudeva and the monks for my mission. The ceremony was given in my honor to empower me with the ability to find the Earthkeeper. It was a long ceremony, in which we went through several symbolic gestures. The part that gave me the most energy was the fire ceremony in which I wrote out my prayer on paper and burned it in the homa fire pit in the center of the temple. I had invited my Kahuna teacher, Serge King, to join me for the ceremony, and he was there with me. The children who had attended the workshop I had given were also there for the Puja. I really found a lot of strength from the children, as they were so positive and supportive of my finding the crystal. I left the ceremony feeling completely confident and supported. I realized that there were literally hundreds of individuals praying and focusing on my journey to find our beloved crystal friend. Directly following the Puja ceremony, I met very briefly with Gurudeva. He asked me to describe to him the size of the Earthkeeper. He held his hand up to his side and said, "Is it this tall?" I held up my hand to show him where the crystal would reach if it were standing next to him.*

*Gurudeva is a very tall person, and the crystal would have come up to the center of his body. I brought my hand up to the point it would reach, and I described to him by using my hands just how tall and wide it was, and how it came to a perfect point. He then said very simply and directly, "I know you have seen the crystal in your mind, and I trust you will know it exactly, and you will find it." He gave me his blessing for the trip, and that was the last I spoke with him before leaving. We had worked together over the past weeks to set up a pyramid system, and had programmed the system using a set of large generator crystals to find the large crystal and bring it home. I know that all of the efforts we made were the reasons my mission was so easy and successful. There is one thing I have been shown over and over again. The bottom line is that it works! There is no magic involved in the power of crystals. By simply using the crystals as tools we can invoke their gifts. Our efforts in programming the large generators to find the Earthkeeper was another one of the many steps we took to help with the project. I know in my heart that without this preparation and support, I could never have gone on such a search. I know that I was given hours of prayer work and support from all of the monks and the devotees of Gurudeva, and never once was I unaware of their efforts. I realize that because I had the vision of the crystal, and that because Gurudeva had been looking for a large crystal for the Iraivan Temple, our paths were divinely crossed to put the pieces together.*

*Before I left the temple, Gurudeva gave me a gift. He handed me a small brown box. Inside I found a very small clear quartz cluster. He told me that he had grown the crystal at the temple over a long period of time. He said, "This is very*

**Gurudeva with The Crystal Lingam**

**Crystal Gurudeva gave me**

(actual size: 1 inch)

special. Take it with you and it will lead you right to the Earthkeeper."

The other part of preparation that I received great motivation from was the visit I made to San Marga the night before I left for Oahu. It was late in the evening, just before sunset. I had gone to the Puja ceremony that morning, bringing with me the offerings I had received, along with my own offerings to leave with the stones on the temple site. That evening, I walked down the path and spent a great deal of time just feeling the energy there. This place is very special to me, and going there is a real treasure. I walked down to the opening and rang the bell three times. I took my time to tune into the vibration of the land. I walked over to the front of the stones and left my offering. As I sat there, I connected with the energy coming from these magnificent stones. I visualized in my mind the large crystal sitting on top of the stones, and worked to connect the energy from my vision with the energy present in the stones. I asked the stones to help me find their long, lost friend and to help me bring him home. I sat there for a long time. Finally, I got up and walked around the grounds in a circular pattern. I experience great peace every time I visit this spot, and always find myself in awe of the energy that is present there. I left San Marga feeling very connected with its vibration, and felt I was able to bring that energy with me on my journey. Many times while I was travelling, I went there in my mind. Even now, I go there in my mind and I rest in this sacred place.

I left Kauai the following morning bound for Oahu. I was to meet with a woman named Rama, who had heard of my work and had asked for me to find a way to spend some time with her. I had called her weeks earlier (once I knew when I was

scheduled to leave Kauai) and I had agreed to spend a day
or so with her on Oahu en route to Arkansas. That evening,
I found myself on Oahu waiting for this person I hadn't yet
met to greet me at the airport.

She arrived fairly late, and while I waited, I spent some
time processing various doubts and fears. What if I couldn't
find her? Where would I stay? Thoughts such as these were
racing through my mind. Silently, I reassured myself that the
Universe doesn't work that way, and that somehow she
would find me. Sure enough, she did. She helped me load
my baggage, and then explained that she had made
arrangements for me to spend the night at the home of a very
close friend of hers where I would be welcome, assuring me
that it was a better spot than what she had to offer. At first I
thought this was rather strange. There I was, once again,
setting out on some unknown destination! But upon arriving
at her friend Dena's house, I soon became extremely
comfortable. I found Dena to be a very warm and friendly
person, and she did make me feel very welcome. We shared
a lot in the short time I stayed with Dena, and became very
close. Although our original connection was very brief, our
cross-purpose eventually unfolded, and our lives have
connected several times since. Dena has grown to be a very
dear friend of mine, and her life has made a complete circle
since I introduced her to the rock reality. I spent the short
time on Oahu working with Rama, Dena, and a small group of
women that were interested in learning more about using
crystals and gems for healing. The connection was a very
powerful one, and I have gone to Oahu since then to continue
sharing information and offering healing work. I left Oahu the
following evening bound for Los Angeles. I arrived there late

in the evening, and was greeted by my dear friend, Kristin. It was great to see her. I hadn't seen her since the previous winter on Kauai. We had met at the store there, and had developed a very wonderful connection. I was so glad to have a friend meet me in L.A., since I am not really fond of large cities. She was driving me several hours by car to where Fred lived. We stopped for a while at a cafe and had some food. I remember sitting there with her and talking about the journey I was about to make to Arkansas, and how miraculous the whole thing had been up to that point. I hadn't talked much to anyone about my inner feelings concerning the task I had somehow agreed to take on. It was really comforting to speak with her. She is an incredibly loving and gentle person, and has always been a reflection of strength and belief for me. She shared much with me in that short time, and gave me a lot of support. When I had revealed to her my vision of the crystal, she offered me only encouragement and the confidence that I would, indeed, find it. Very few people had really known the degree of anticipation going on inside of me at that time-taking the journey, not knowing how I was going to actually pull it off, and so on. Sharing my vision with her in detail somehow made it all seem easy. Spending this time with Kristin and receiving her support turned out to be a very important step along the way for me. We arrived at Fred's house and he welcomed us in. Kristin stayed for a few minutes, but was anxious to start the drive home. Fred took me to a room downstairs, where he said I could sleep. I broke out in laughter when I saw the enormous crystal clusters that were crowding the room. I said, "You don't really think I'll get any sleep here, do you?" Needless to say, I spent the night in a heightened state. I certainly wouldn't call it sleep! It was a state of rest, however. I was very much awake, but at the same time, I was receiving a renewal of my energy. I was amazed at how great I felt in the morning. Well, at last we were Arkansas-bound. Fred's wife took us to the airport and we flew to Texas, changed planes, and then proceeded to Little Rock, Arkansas. A young man (who was a friend of Fred's) met us at the airport and then drove us to Jessieville, where we had a place waiting for us to stay. It was early evening by the time we arrived. I got my belongings and set up my room. One of the first things I did was to set up an altar, for I felt a strong need to center in and to get ready for the reality of the journey I was on. Later that evening, my first night in Arkansas, I sat down before the altar I had prepared. I lit a candle, said a prayer, and asked for help and guidance. I sat silently in meditation, waiting for any message that would come to me. I received only one answer, which was that I was to share my truth as clearly as I could-my whole truth-and I was not to leave out any part.

I examined this message very carefully, and what I arrived at was pretty simple. It was clear to me that I needed to share the details of my vision of the crystal, why I was in Arkansas, and the purpose and final destination for the crystal. After considering this, I realized that whoever it was that had possession of the crystal would either connect with my truth, or tell me I was out to lunch. Either way, I had to follow my guidance. Therefore, I did.

The first morning I was in Arkansas, I was scheduled to meet with Fred and his connection to look at crystals to purchase. Up to this point, the only clear detail I had been given as to where I was to find the crystal had come in a very vague message. I was simply told that I would find my own connection, and that it would not be the person that Fred was taking me to.

I arrived about half an hour before I was supposed to meet with Fred. As I waited in front of the place we were to meet, I was pulled, instead, to the other side of the street, where there was a large store selling crystals. As I walked to the front of the building, there, right in front of me stood the largest single crystal I had ever seen. It was very rough and was simply being used as a yard display. I thought to myself, "Well, I'm definitely on the right track!" I went inside, walked up to the counter, and began talking to the woman who worked there. I introduced myself to her, and told her immediately why I was in Arkansas. I asked her if she knew anyone who might have a very large, single-pointed crystal, somewhat like the one outside, but larger. She took down my name and the number where I was staying at. She told me that she wasn't aware of him having any large crystals, but if anyone could possibly help me it would be Jimmy Coleman. I thanked her sincerely for any help she could give me and asked her to please let Mr. Coleman know that I would like to see him. I then walked back outside and across the street to meet with Fred and his friend. I spent several hours in this large warehouse of crystals, selecting those I wished to buy. It was a very intense process. I had never been in a room with so many crystals. I was glad that I had brought my gem silica with me because I could feel the drain on my system from being in this room with so many crystals. When I first got there, I met a man named Greg. He introduced himself to me as the only person there that was into the metaphysical side of the crystals. We got along great, and had an immediate understanding between us. I asked him if he knew of anyone who might have a very large, clear quartz crystal. I explained to him that I had come from Kauai to find a certain crystal. He immediately told me that large crystals had not been found in Arkansas, but that he knew of a man named Gary Fleck who had a large crystal from Africa, and that he could take me to see him. I said that I was already aware of that crystal, as Gurudeva had contacted Gary years earlier when he first decided to find a large crystal for the temple he was going to build. Gurudeva and I had discussed the importance of finding a crystal from the United States, and this particular crystal had been transported from Africa. At this point, Greg told me that I wasn't going to find any large crystal here, but he wished me luck. I met with Greg many times while I was in Arkansas, and we became very good friends. Later on, he was to be very instrumental in making some very wonderful crystals available to me, one of which would be my first lazer wand.

The word had travelled fast to Jimmy that a woman from Hawaii was looking for a very large crystal. I received word later on that afternoon that he had brought out crystals for me to see, and at what time I could come to view them.

I rode up to Jimmy's house with my friend, Dale Long, who had driven from California to help me while I was in Arkansas. Dale is a close friend who I met on Kauai. He had left Kauai the month before I did, and was very supportive of me and the mission I was on. We arrived at Jimmy's warehouse late that afternoon, and we were taken to a room that was a lot like a garage. The yard in front of the building was completely filled with quartz crystals. The crystals had been brought here carefully wrapped in newspaper, unwrapped, allowed to dry, and then processed to remove the red clay they are found in. I was in heaven. I had never seen so many crystals in one place before.

One of the people that worked for Jimmy took me over to the room where the crystals Jimmy had brought out for me to see were located. He slid open a large door, and there before me appeared two very big crystals. I stood in silence for a moment, completely in shock. Tears started to fill my eyes and began falling down my face. I walked over to the crystal directly in front of me and kneeled down. I placed my hands on the crystal. I knew immediately that this was the crystal I had seen in my vision. We had been united! Many thoughts flashed through my mind. I wasn't aware of anyone or anything else in the room, and the others with me seemed to sense my departure. Before I had left Kauai, Gurudeva had given me a small, clear quartz cluster. He had told me that it would bring me right to the crystal I had seen in my mind. Needless to say, I had kept this small cluster with me, all safe in a small box. Kneeling there with tears on my face, I took the small box from my purse and removed the crystal. I knew that Gurudeva's crystal would confirm whether or not this was the crystal that was to come home with me. If they were not compatible there would be an obvious rejection, somewhat similar to placing north-to-north together on two magnets. I carefully placed the small cluster on the tip of the large crystal. Right as the two touched, I saw a white flash. There was definitely a connection-a locking of the two, as if they were somehow related. This was all the confirmation I needed. I realized now that the final test was before me — meeting the man who owned this sacred rock, telling him my story, and somehow getting this crystal home to Kauai. I sat there for who knows how long, for I was in my own world, alone with an ancient friend. I put my ear to the crystal to hear what it wanted to say to me. The message that came through loud and clear was, "Peace, peace. I'm here to bring peace!" I leaned over, embraced the stone, and whispered to it, "Well friend, you have to help me get you home to Kauai. Please help me now." By this time all eyes were upon me, and as I stood up, someone started asking me, "Well, is that the one, is this it?" I don't know if it was the smile on my face or the joy in my being that gave me away, but somehow the others had gotten the message. I was temporarily mesmerized. I was also in deep thought, preparing for my next step-sharing my truth, my message, with Jimmy. I heard someone speak, telling me to come because Jimmy was on his way down from his house. He had just returned from the mine and had gone home for a shower. I bent down and picked up the cluster that was sitting on the tip of the crystal. I joined the others walking towards Jimmy, who was coming down the road.

Meeting Jimmy Coleman was again a step into my past, my soul-lives.

He stood before me, this very large man. I felt very comfortable with his energy, and the gentleness coming through him was incredible. I looked directly into his eyes and told him my name, and then I began very slowly telling him my story. I left out not a detail, and shared with him the vision and the complete process that had brought me to him. I explained to him where the crystal was going and the importance of putting crystals like these in places where they could do their service to humanity. I expressed the wondrous fact to him that the crystal was exactly as it had appeared in my vision, and that seeing it before me had truly blown my mind. I found with each word I spoke an understanding between us. It was very easy for me to speak with him. As I stood there, again I was in my own world, unaware of the others waiting for me, or anything else happening. All that mattered to me was sharing my truth with Jimmy and communicating the importance of the mission I had come on. I know we stood there for a long time. I felt a very peaceful, powerful presence in him, and an incredible familiar feeling with him. I knew, surely, that we had been together before, and later on in our relationship he shared that he had felt the same. Once I had completed telling him my story, I simply asked him if he would make the crystal available to me, and how much he would like to receive for it. He looked directly into my eyes with a very loving compassion and told me the price. I said that was fine, and that I would get in touch with Gurudeva to make the arrangements to complete the transaction. I asked him to please give me a day or so, and I would get right back to him. I thanked him, and I expressed my gratitude for the work he was doing. I have a very deep respect for Jimmy, and find him to be among the few who are truly devoted to the higher purpose of the crystal work being done on the earth. My respect runs very deep for him, as I got to know him again while I was there. I found a man who is in tune with the Earth Mother and the crystals. The ability to remove these giants from the earth is a stupendous feat.

I left Jimmy's that day on a high I had never experienced before. It took me about twenty-four hours to get through to anyone at the temple. I found out later that they were involved in a special ceremony (Guru Purnima) for Gurudeva. This ceremony is held once a year on the full moon in July, where all Hindus pay respect to their Guru. No one was answering the phone. Finally, I got through to Ceyon Swami. I simply told him that I had found the crystal, and described it to him. I told him it was exactly as I had seen it, and that it was incredible. I also told him the price. He asked me if I could please send him some pictures so they could see it. I said okay, and that I would take the pictures and air-express them over. I told him I would call back in two days or so, and left it at that. Jimmy and I got together that evening and took a roll of pictures, got them developed, and I expressed them to Kauai. It takes fourty-eight hours to get anything to Hawaii via UPS. So, once I knew that the pictures had arrived, I called Ceyon Swami. I spoke to Ceyon and I could feel his excitement over the phone. He asked me to make arrangements with Jimmy to secure the crystal, and said that he would be sending me a deposit for the crystal until they could raise the rest of the funds. I said that I would relate the information to Jimmy, and Ceyon asked me to call him back with information on where to wire the funds. A day or so went by, and again I called Ceyon to give him the information as to where to wire the funds in Jessieville. By this time, Ceyon was really excited, and he told me that they had already acquired all the funds and that he was sending me the complete amount so that I could just pay for the crystal and get it on its way home. This didn't come as a suprise. I knew that things would happen quickly, and I felt strongly that the reason things were coming together in such a short time had a lot to do with the upcoming Harmonic Convergence. I knew that the crystal needed to be on Kauai for this event. I later found out that Gurudeva had the same feeling as to the importance of the crystal being on Kauai at the time of the convergence. I was so glad to hear that it had all come together. I was ecstatic. I made the arrangements to have Ceyon wire the funds to me. I told Jimmy that we had been able to raise all the money, and that he could get the crystal ready to ship to Kauai. Once the funds had arrived, I went up to meet with Jimmy. He had built a crate for the crystal and was ready to send it off. I went with him to where the crate was situated, and he insisted on opening it up to show me that, indeed, the crystal was safely inside. I told him I had complete trust in him, and it wasn't necessary for him to do that, and I laughed. Needless to say, there, all cozy inside the crate, was my beloved crystal friend. Jimmy asked me to go with him to the shipping location. I said I would be glad to. We got a large truck and put it in the back. Our first stop was at a place where they sold the metal strips that go around the crate. I was enjoying participating in all the steps necessary to get the crystal home. We secured the crate with these metal bands, and then drove into town to where the shipping company was. The crystal was to go by truck to the nearest shipping port, and then would travel by barge to Oahu, and then on to Kauai. This would take approximately six weeks. We did the necessary paperwork and payed for the crystal to be delivered directly to the temple on Kauai. (Having lived in Hawaii for over twelve years, I knew it would be nearly impossible for it to get through to Kauai without some form of mix-up. So, I did all that was physically possible to make it clear and easy as far as the shipping arrangements were concerned). Jimmy and I then carefully backed the truck into the area where we would unload the crate and take it off the truck. This part was very intense. First we had to get the truck through the entrance, which took both of us working together. I helped outside by directing him and he, of course, drove the truck in. Then we very carefully lowered the crate onto the floor where it awaited the trip home. It was now physically out of my hands. I said my farewells to my crystal friend, and experienced an immense feeling of relief. At last my mission was completed. Finally, the crystal which had appeared to me in my visions, was on its way to Kauai. It's hard to express in words what I felt like at that moment. It had been two and a half years of work since I first received the vision of the crystal and experienced all the events leading to our joyful union. I felt an encompassing sense of peace within myself. This peace came in the form of gratitude for being able to complete the work I had been given. Overall, I guess I could say that this sense of relief was the thing that gave me the most joy. The entire experience had been overwhelming and quite unbelievable. I'm continually amazed at how the Universe works to assist us once we have the faith to step out and go for it. Jimmy and I left, and returned to Jessieville. At this point, I had only one more thing I felt I needed to do while I was in Arkansas, which was to complete the third reason I had been given to go to Arkansas — the healing and balancing for the earth.

It was through my friendship with Jimmy that the third purpose for my trip to Arkansas was revealed. I felt a great deal of appreciation for him, and wanted in some way to give him a gift, an offering, a showing of this gratitude. I had heard of a mine that had collapsed, and as things unfolded between us, he shared with me more of himself and his work. I learned of the details of the mine, and of the incredible crystals that had come from the mine before it had fallen in. He showed me the cluster that he had removed from the mine,

and shared with me his understanding. He said he felt that
the earth was a lot like a woman-one needs to court her and
show her their love. He said that he felt the energy wasn't
right, and that the mine had given enough. She just plain had
no more to give. Later on during the week it was shown to me
that this was how I could express my appreciation, and that
the healing work I had been asked to perform before I left
Kauai was to be at this mine. I allowed the Universe to unfold
the perfect path for me to complete this, and sure enough,
I was taken right to it. It came from my friend, Greg. One day
we were discussing the mine and how it had fallen in. I
asked him if he would please take me there, as I needed to do
some work with the earth, and to make some offerings.
I explained to him how I had been given three reasons for
coming to Arkansas, and that the third one had finally been
revealed to me. I explained to Greg that this was a way for
me to show my appreciation to Jimmy, as my words weren't
enough. So one afternoon, Greg took me to the mine and left
me alone as I did my work. I walked down deep inside the
opening that had been carved in the earth, and I brought some
flowers and a bunch of rose quartz. I left these at the spot
where the mine had collapsed. I then walked back up to the
top of the mountain area above the mine and proceeded with
my energy healing. This was done in the form of a ceremony
involving chanting and praying, a ceremony where I dance
and do a lot of chanting and gesturing with my hands and
arms. I work directly with my spirit guides and bring through
plenty of light and energy, offering it directly to the earth. It is
a very powerful form of prayer for me, and each time I have
done such a ceremony, the energy that has come through has
been simply magnificent. I took a long time in connecting

49

directly with the energy at this spot so that I could continue working from a long distance later on. Over the three-year period since I was at the mine, I have gone back many times to continue with my healing work. I spoke with Jimmy once I had done my work, and I told him that I had done it for him, and I would continue working with that spot until the energy was balanced so he could complete his work there. He was very glad I had been able to tune into where the work was needed, and there seemed to be an unspoken understanding between us about the whole subject. I did express to him where I felt the imbalance had originated, and offered him what I felt would be a solution for avoiding any future problems. Jimmy is one of a few people who can mine the crystals with respect and consideration, and I felt it very necessary for him to either do the mining in that spot alone, or to seek out another person who was in harmony with the energy there, and the sacredness of the process. I spoke with him on the phone about two months ago, and I shared with him that I had been checking in on the mine, and that I felt it was getting very close to opening up to him again. We talked then about my feeling for him to find the right person to work with, and he understood completely. I have remained close to Jimmy. Our friendship is very sacred to me, and I know our connection is an eternal one.

Now that I had truly finished with the three reasons for my journey to Arkansas, it was nearly time for me to go home. I spent the remainder of the week enjoying the people, and visited the mines several times to look for crystals. I truly fell in love with Arkansas and the folks who live there. In a way, I could have stayed forever. But finally, it was really time for me to go. I made the rounds, saying goodbye to the friends I had made. My friend, Dale, was driving me to the airport, and I asked him to please take me up to Jimmy's so that I could say goodbye to him. This was the hardest part of the whole trip. I had found a long, lost friend in Jimmy, and I knew that I was going to really miss him. I walked up to him and stood there for a long time. I told him, once again, how much he meant to me, and that I was eternally grateful for the work he was doing. I found it hard to express my gratitude for his help in finding the crystal. Jimmy gave me a big hug and simply said to me, "Now girl, don't stay away so long this time, okay?" There seemed to be an unspoken bond between us, and the final words he spoke to me confirmed my first feelings of reuniting with an old soul-friend. Dale drove me to the airport, and once again I found myself having to say goodbye. Dale had been a tremendous support for me, and to this day I feel that he is truly one of my guardian angels.

At last I was reunited with my family. They greeted me at the Seattle airport, and we drove north to our home. Slowly, I began settling back into my personal life and the projects that needed my attention. Many times over in the following weeks I received messages from my crystal friend. I'm continually amazed at the connection we have, and it seems that distance is no obstacle in our ability to communicate. I had spoken with Ceyon several times about the actual day the crystal was due to arrive. I had made arrangements for the crystal to be delivered directly to the temple headquarters. It was at the point where the crystal reached Oahu that it was lost. I had a strong feeling that this was going to happen, and wasn't too alarmed when Ceyon told me that they couldn't find it en route, and didn't know where it was. I took a few minutes to connect with the crystal and locate it in my mind.

*I then got on the phone and called the transportation company
and got through to the person handling it on Oahu. I was able
to talk him through the confusion of where it was supposed to
be, and where it really was. I knew that it was already there
on the dock, although he kept telling me that it never came in.
Finally I assured him that it was somewhere in Oahu,
specifically at the receiving center, and would be loaded on a
barge and sent to Kauai. This gentleman finally followed my
guidance and went to look for the crystal where I had told him
it was. Sure enough, there it was, waiting to be loaded onto
the barge for Kauai. He explained to me that they only ship
to Kauai on certain days, and that it would be leaving on the
next scheduled barge run to Kauai. I called Ceyon to let him
know that I had located the crystal, and when he could expect
it to arrive. The next complication that occurred was in the
payment for shipping. The gentleman on Oahu insisted that
the fee was to be paid on delivery. I assured him that the fee
had been paid in full when I sent the crystal from Arkansas.
He couldn't find record of this, and was very uncooperative.
I got on the phone once again and called the company who
had shipped the crystal from Arkansas to Oahu. I got the
invoice number and all of the necessary information to prove
that I had already paid. I called Oahu once again and gave
the man this information. At last he was satisfied with the
fact that the shipping had been paid, and he agreed to deliver
the crystal as scheduled. After all of this confusion, the
crystal was finally sent off to Kauai, and arrived for the
Harmonic Convergence. As you can well imagine, this brought
me great joy. I spent the day of the convergence at the ocean
on the coast of Washington, while hundreds gathered at the
temple with my beloved crystal friend. Afterwards, I received*

numerous phone calls from friends on Kauai who had been to see the crystal. Everyone was amazed. I wasn't on Kauai until three months later, when I was able to go see the crystal at the temple. It was a wonderful experience to see it standing upright, beaming its radiant, green aura. The crystal and I still communicate often. It speaks loud and clear to me no matter where I am. I am very anxious to see the vision through to its final phase, which will consist of the installment of the crystal inside the Iraivan Temple at the San Marga Sanctuary. I cannot express strongly enough just how important this is. Once the crystal is located on this ancient power spot, I know it can truly begin its service to humanity. I also know that this crystal is a very important tool for the healing of the planet and the vision of peace for mankind. I am truly blessed to have been a part of it all, and I am devoted to doing all I can to see the temple completed as soon as possible. The Iraivan Temple is being built entirely on donations from the people of the world. This temple will be open to all people, regardless of their personal religious paths. I would like to encourage folks to get involved in the temple-building process. If you would like to do so, please contact: The Church of San Marga, Post Office Box 1030, Kapaa, Hawaii * 96746. If you would like to visit the temple and see the crystal, please call in advance to arrange a time. One needs to realize that the current location is a spiritual monastery, and people should not just arrive expecting to see the crystal. Please call (808) 822-0080. You will find the monks very pleasant, and willing to accommodate you.

Scale model

of

# The Iraivan Temple

Chapter Three

# A Crystal Temple

A white granite temple, handcarved in India and shipped to Kauai.
Positioned on an ancient Lemurian power spot and housing
the 39-inch, 700 pound super-crystal, also known as the
Swayambhu Siva Lingam.

*One asks why we need to build a temple that will cost
millions of dollars. With the poverty of the world and the
homeless, let us remember that our souls and spirits also
need a home. Where in today's large cities can one go to find
a resting place? Surrounded by man's materialism in the form
of shopping centers and other creations to entertain our
worldly ways, we continually build larger cities, more exotic
entertainment centers, and the like. But again, when one
needs to understand their own spiritual quest, where can they
go? Our churches are locked, except for a few hours on a
certain day of the week, and there one finds a form of
spirituality handed to them. In this current world of ours with
its unique challenges, there is a desperate need for a
sanctuary, a place of peace where one can go regardless of
what day of the week or what hour of the day it is, a place
where one can sit alone and reach out to understand their
own unique connection with God, a place for all the people of
the world to pray. Along with the need to feed the hungry and
house the homeless, one needs to see the necessity of creating
places of peace for our spirits, removed from the confusion of
the worldly creations, leaving us free to seek other levels of*

understanding. We need to address the hungry spirits and the homeless souls wandering in the world, confused about the very pressing issues of creation, purpose, and existence. We need a place that is focused entirely on addressing these issues, a place that will not discriminate against one's understanding of God, or the way one chooses to communicate with God. Our needs are for a temple of light devoted to the people of the planet, centered and created with love and harmony for all of mankind, and united with the common goal of peace.

Imagine, if you will, a path wandering through a meadow and continuing down through beautiful flower gardens, a path laid of granite slabs that will wind through the Pavillion of Religions and on through the Meditation Gardens. Imagine, then, your expression as you complete your journey on the path to stand before a solid white granite temple composed of 3.2 million pounds of stone, along with 343 tons of concrete centered on a foundation thirty-five feet wide, one hundred feet long, and four feet high. Picture, again, your reaction as you enter the temple to see, standing there before you, the world's largest single-pointed crystal lingam sitting peacefully centered in a solid silver base, positioned as the focal point for the temple.

"Imagine yourself seated on the top of the world,
Cool white Indian stones beneath you,
A smooth granite pillar against your back,
As soft Hawaiian breezes waft through your hair,
And the fragrance of jasmine floats in the air
-that is Iraivan!
Imagine the rustling of palm trees in the trades,
Ancient sounds of temple bells and conches calling,
Your mind expanding into infinite space,
While a sacred river wanders by a holy place.
-that is Iraivan!"
—*Taken from the San Marga Newsletter, May, 1990.*

*Please receive the following information as a guide to better understand the San Marga project. I will be giving various details that will help one to get a better picture of the crystal temple that is currently being built on the Island of Kauai.*

*The original beginning for the San Marga Spiritual Sanctuary came to Gurudeva (Sivaya Subramuniyaswami) in February of 1975 through a series of mystical visions. San Marga literally means "the straight path to God realization". The plans for the development of the property were also given in these visions. The area that is currently being developed has been a spiritual site for thousands of years. The first Hawaiian priest, Kuamo'o Mo'okini, came to Kauai in 480 c.e. {common era (or a.d.)} and established temples along the river. He named what is now the San Marga Sanctuary, "Pihanakalani, where heaven and earth meet."*

*It's interesting to know that there was a time when Hawaii was ruled by Kings, and that certain areas on the mountain and at the spiritual centers were only available to the royalty. If you had desired to visit the San Marga Spiritual Sanctuary during this era (unless you were among this royal group), it would not have been possible. In the early 1900's, it was a theosophy center, and in 1969 the property was acquired by Gurudeva. Along with the vision of San Marga came the declaration that it would be the place where the world comes to pray. The visions of San Marga came like the vision of the large crystal, unbidden. Psychic visions are not from one's imagination, nor are they dreams.*

*The Iraivan temple, which will stand at the center of the San Marga Sanctuary, will be thirty-five feet tall. Iraivan will be America's first stone temple composed of white granite. Granite is about fifty percent crystal, and is a very strong substance. It is predicated to stand for over one thousand years as a place of worship for many generations to come. The Hindu word, Iraivan, means "the all-pervasive one who is worshipped".*

*The design for the temple has come from a stapathi from India. A stapathi is a temple designer who comes from a lineage of temple builders handed down through the Vedic tradition. V. Ganapati Stapathi is the man who has designed the Iraivan Temple. He comes from a family in Southern India that has built temples for a thousand years. He has designed this temple to incorporate divine architectural knowledge to properly utilize the spiritual power of the two swayambhu (naturally formed) Siva Lingams (identifying marks or symbols representing God), the great stone that appeared to Gurudeva in his original vision where Lord Siva was sitting and the Earthkeeper crystal that first appeared to me in a vision. The main structure of this temple will be carved in India, and then* shipped to Kauai. One of the truly unique features in the design of the Iraivan Temple is that the structure will be built directly above the existing sacred stones which are the remnants of an ancient Hawaiian heau (temple). The central stone that holds the spiritual ray hooked deep into the earth will be connected to the Crystal Lingam through a column containing threads of copper, silver, and gold. The two Lingams will then work together, greatly intensifying the already powerful vortex.

The Crystal Lingam is a naturally formed stone that has self-healed. This means that when the crystal was broken off from the rock it was growing on, and as it laid there, the bottom of the crystal started to grow again. It is believed that the crystal was broken off from the rock base during a major earth shift. This gives us what is known as a self-healed crystal. It is very similar to being a naturally formed, double-terminated crystal, except where there would be one single termination there are, instead, several hundred. I found this fact about the crystal very symbolic when I first discovered it during my visit to Arkansas. The properties of a self-healed crystal give the crystal the ability to send and receive energy from both ends, like that of a double-terminated one. It also amplifies the natural healing abilities of the stone, and gives it extraordinary healing properties. One needs to simply sit in its presence to receive this healing energy. I know that once the crystal is in place within the Iraivan Temple and activated, it will bring miraculous healing energies, both to individuals who are in its presence and to the earth (amplified through the natural stone below it, and then into the core of the earth itself). At the same time, because of its unique formation and ability to access

59

# Beloved
# Gurudeva

*energy from both directions, it will also become an antenna for universal information and will broadcast to anyone who has the ability to hear what it is saying. The importance of getting this temple built as soon as possible is critical for the times that are ahead of us. This temple is an important part of the progress for mankind. All people of the earth, whether or not they ever go to the Iraivan Temple, will be blessed once this temple is completed.*

*The following passage is a message from Gurudeva:*

**"There is no greater thing to do on earth than to build a temple. You, too, can become and continue to be a temple builder."**

**All my life I have been a temple builder, and we are happy to say that we now have ten temples and shrines and have started the worship in many others in the United States, Canada, and Great Britain. A temple is the wellspring of life. It is a place of "higher consciousness". A temple is the home of God. "To build a temple is the greatest thing that one can do while on earth. A spiritual vortex is a place where the inner world connects with the physical world. Every temple is a vortex of its own kind. San Marga is one of the several great ones on this planet. Come walk San Marga with me, and feel for yourself the healing energies of higher consciousness at the Iraivan Temple site."**

*– Taken from the June/July '89 Iraivan Temple Newsletter.*

*The Iraivan Temple is being built entirely from donations from the people of the world. The donations come in different forms. For some they are a spontaneous love offering. Others give as an act of self-denial. Self-denial is the act of not doing something for oneself, and giving the funds that would have*

61

*otherwise gone for non-holy work. There are still others who give a pledge of a certain amount on a monthly or yearly basis. Once one gives a donation, they receive a monthly newsletter and are kept informed of the progress of the temple building. I'm personally glad to be a part of the dedicated individuals who are committed to building the temple. I believe that by participating in this holy work, one's soul is blessed and positive karma is created. I encourage you to become a temple builder and to have the joy of knowing that you are helping to create a very special place for the people of the earth. Please understand that even as this temple is being built according to Hindu tradition, it is being recognized as a universal temple available to anyone, regardless of their personal faith. There are plans for a Pavilion of Religions on the San Marga Sanctuary, where all faiths will be honored.*

*I often think about the millions of dollars in the world that are used for various things. I find it hard to believe the things that we spend money on. I see hotels and shopping centers being built to attract more material gain, and I think what a blessing it would be to have just one percent of what is spent on such projects to help build the Iraivan Temple. Then I think about the many individuals who have millions of dollars and don't even know what to do with all of it. And then I see, little by little, many more souls becoming devoted to building the Iraivan Temple. It comes in donations of five dollars here, and fifty dollars there. Slowly, yet surely, it will all manifest. It takes a strong desire on all our parts to want it to happen, and then it does happen.*

*I know that in my own life, the Iraivan Temple has caused a great change in my awareness of financial matters. I have gone into the center of my being to take a look at my* relationship with money, to get clear with my ability to manifest, and to feel good about it. Being raised with a very materialistic father, I had to start all over again with how I felt about money. I now see money as a tool that can help create wonderful spiritual centers and to free mankind on a level that was never clear to me in the past. I'm truly grateful to the vision of San Marga and the temple building project. I kept meditating on what I could do to help raise more money. My own financial situation has been a struggle, and I haven't been able to give much. This was disturbing to me, as my spirit and heart are one hundred percent into building this temple. The more I focused, the more I wanted to do something to help. It was this desire that gave me the inspiration to write and publish this book. In this way, I am hoping to make a larger contribution than I could have on my own. This is why I have pledged one-half of all profits to the general building fund for the Iraivan Temple. I am glad this project exists, and I already feel the blessing in my own personal relationship with money. I am now working consciously to become better at manifesting, and feel that money has taken on a new meaning in my life. This, in itself, is really great. I no longer feel boxed in to someone else's values or reasons to have money. Thank you, Iraivan! There is a donation form included at the end of this chapter for anyone who would like to become a temple builder. Feel free to write the monks if you have any questions or seek any additional information. I can't find adequate words to express my gratitude to all those who are helping to build the Iraivan Temple. I'll leave it with MAHALO (a Hawaiian word for grateful thanks).

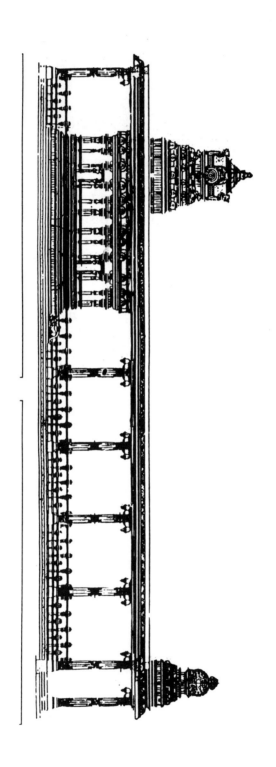

# I'm a Temple Builder!

## Here's My Contribution to Make Iraivan a Reality!

**Quantity of Stone You Are Sponsoring:**

I am enclosing $ _____ for _____ pounds of stone.

**Nature of Contribution:** *(Please check the appropriate box.)*

☐ Self-denial contribution ☐ Spontaneous love offering
☐ Monthly pledge ☐ Monthly tithe
☐ Other: _____

Name: _____

Address: _____

City, state, zip: _____

Phone: _____

VISA/MC#: _____ Expiration date: _____

Signature: _____

Please charge a regular monthly donation of $ _____ to my credit card account for the period of _____ to _____.

*All donations are tax deductible in the United States.*

---

**The Church of San Marga**

Post Office Box 1030
Kapaa, Hawaii • 96746 USA
Phone (808) 822-0080
Fax: (808) 822-4351

### About the San Marga Project

The story of the San Marga spiritual sanctuary—of rolling meadows, meditation paths, a pavilion of religion, rudraksha tree forest and sacred shrines—was first revealed in mystic vision to Gurudeva Sivaya Subramuniyaswami in 1975. At the end of the path stood the crown jewel—Iraivan Temple—a glistening, white stone edifice which would enshrine the world's largest single-pointed *spadika* (quartz crystal) *Sivalingam*. Slowly the vision is manifesting, Iraivan will be the first Hindu temple in America constructed entirely of stone—carved in India from white granite, shipped to Hawaii's Garden Island and assembled on San Marga. Donations are coming in daily from seekers around the world. One thousand years from now, when other structures have long since crumbled, Iraivan (literally, "He who is worshipped") will remain as a living testimony of the timeless Self, God, within each soul. You can share in this long-enduring, holy effort. Each contribution is translated into a quantity of finished stone at the rate of $5 per pound, including shipping to Hawaii. Give generously and come to San Marga soon!

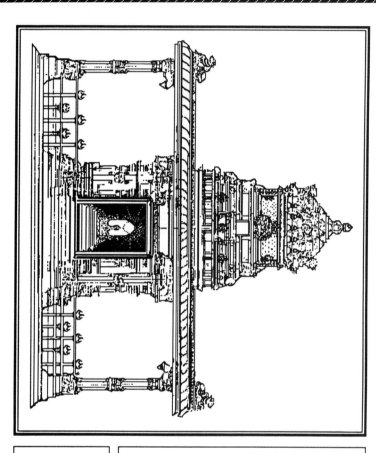

## Currency Exchange

One pound of stone
can be sponsored for:

| | |
|---|---|
| United States | US$6.50 |
| Australian | A$6.50 |
| British | £7.95 |
| Canadian | $5.90 |
| Fijian | $7.60 |
| French | fr31.35 |
| German | Dm9.25 |
| Hong Kong | HK$39.05 |
| Indian | Rs84.00 |
| Japanese | ¥710.00 |
| Malaysian | M$13.50 |
| Mauritius | Rs78.00 |
| Singapore | S$9.80 |
| Sri Lanka | Rs198.00 |
| Taiwan | NT$129.00 |

Introduced to the
San Marga Project and
sponsored by:

Armida Press

**Makana Mountain, North Shore of Kauai**

Chapter Four

# Kauai Speaks

It was fifteen years ago that Kauai called my name and I made my
first journey to this sacred place.

*I owe my awareness of Kauai to an old friend named Eric,
who I knew from Bellingham. I had decided to take a trip
during the winter and couldn't decide where I should go.
Eric had spent time on Kauai and was telling me about this
ancient valley on the north shore of the Island. The name of
the valley was Kalalau, and when he first said the name, it
was like an alarm went off inside of my soul. I had never
had any desire to go to Hawaii as my perception of it, until
this point, was an overcrowded tourist destination. Eric was
instrumental in getting me to Kauai. As he talked about this
Island, I knew that it was different from the Hawaii that was
being presented on another level. He described the trail to
this ancient valley and how one could experience what
Hawaii was truly all about: beauty, nature, rainbows, warm
ocean and secluded beaches. It was a chance to become one
with God's creation and be with myself. I listened to
everything Eric told me and from that moment on, I was
overcome with this passion to go to Kauai, to place my bare
feet upon this ancient trail and walk to the valley known as
Kalalau.*

*Several months had passed before I was able to get it
together to go to Kauai. At that time, I was living in a cabin*

with a woman named Prema Priya, in the backwoods of Lake Samish. We lived in an old log cabin without any electricity and just cold running water, which sat on top of a hill where the road, accessible by foot only, ends.

It was during my stay with this woman that I was introduced to meditation and yoga, and I was given an opportunity to address my spiritual path. Prema Priya was on a spiritual path with a Guru from India. I know now that she was a Hindu, but at that time I wasn't aware of this. She lived a very structured life. Her day began at five thirty in the morining and she performed yoga and meditations throughout the day. This particular time in my life was very symbolic to me. She never forced her way of life on me, and gave me complete acceptance. I experienced this as unconditional love, and I'll have to admit that it was one of the first times I had encountered it. I chose to participate in the meditation and yoga excercise. I went to her classes at the college and got involved of my own free will. What she offered me was very instrumental in opening the door to my spiritual understanding. It took me a long time to get it together as far as meditation was concerned, as I had a hard time getting my mind to be still. Prema Priya taught all of her classes for free and never asked me for anything. I respect her as a priestess, and am eternally grateful for all that she shared with me.

During my stay with her, I was trying to decide where to go. I was torn in several directions; part of me wanted to go to Kauai and part of me wanted to go to Tennessee to visit "The Farm". Not being able to make up my mind, I finally decided to consult the I Ching and to seek the guidance of the ancient oracle. I took out my yarrow sticks and went through the procedure to receive some guidance on the matter. The message was very clear: "Now is the time to cross the great water." With no water between here and Tennessee, that left me only one direction to go. I knew that I must go to Kauai immediately and journey to Kalalau valley. In my heart, I was really tired of being alone and I was searching for a place where I could go and be free to experiece my inner quest. The people who were my friends at that time were in an old mind set and everyone wanted to hold me back. I had been going through some very powerful experiences with visions and receiving information. I wanted to be where I could figure it all out for myself, away from the protective eye of my group of friends. Please remember that fifteen years ago, people who were visionary or psychic were classified as crazy and completely written off as "out-to-lunch". I know now that my being called to Kalalau Valley at that particular time in my life was a turning point for me-a chance to be able to come into my own personal power. I'm still grateful to that part of me which was brave enough to go for it.

It was the first week in January when I left Seattle for Kauai. I arrived on Oahu at two o'clock a.m. and had to spend the rest of the morning in the airport. There were no connecting flights to Kauai until around seven o'clock a.m. That was a very uncomfortable night. Finally, my flight had arrived and I headed for Kauai. By this time, I was really tired. I hailed a taxi and arrived at a hotel in Kapaa, spending only one night there. I then decided to backpack and camp on the island for the remainder of my stay.

I found a park I wanted to camp at and ended up spending some time there. I found a wonderful family of campers at the park and we all had a great time. One morning, as I walked

71

by the river and watched it meet the sea, it somehow spoke to me. I felt this calling to go to Kalalau. I'll never forget this feeling, as I have experienced it several times since then. Each time I receive this calling, I can't resist the urge within me to go there.

The next morning I packed up everything and headed for the north shore to find the trail that would lead me to Kalalau Valley. In those days, it was fairly easy to hitchhike. Sometimes I had to wait a long time, but I always got to where I was going. I was given a ride by some tourists all the way to the end of the road where the trail begins. As I began the walk, little did I know that the hike was as difficult as it was. (We're talking advanced hiking here.) I had decided I was going to walk barefoot. So I did.

I reached the first valley known as Hanakapiai before sunset and set up my camp. This was the first time I had gone hiking alone. Eric had told me all about the trail and he had expressed the importance of hiking alone the first time to Kalalau. He told me that it was a very sacred place, and that during ancient times, only the high priests were able to go there and walk the trail on the night of the full moon. Well, I was glad not to be there during that time because doing it by myself in the daylight was a big enough challenge for me. The other thing happening to me at that time was that I was doing a fast from food, and was only drinking liquids.

I spent the night in Hanakapai and headed out for Kalalau early the next morning. Well, things started to go downhill from there. Walking barefoot was great, but the pack I was carrying was much too heavy. I hadn't considered the trail to be so difficult, and should have thought to store a lot of the possessions I didn't need before starting out. I reached the second valley, which is a six-mile hike up and down incredible mountain sides, winding in and out of the Napali coastline. Hanakoa is the second valley, and the half-way mark to Kalalau Valley. This was as far as I made it during my first attempt at the trip.

By the time I reached this second valley, I was having some serious problems. First of all, because I was walking barefoot, my feet were so torn up from a green, thorny plant, which had been placed onto slippery areas by other people who had walked the trail. Not being able to clean and care for my feet properly, I acquired a staff infection. Staff is a serious problem in the tropics, as the warm air helps it to grow. Along with this problem, I had not eaten anything and I was having a difficult time keeping my energy up. After spending a few days camping at Hanakoa Valley, I decided to turn back so I could give my feet a chance to heal and find some place to stash all the extra stuff to lighten my pack. I felt this was the best thing to do considering how I was feeling.

I was sitting on the large rocks in the center of the river listening to the water flow when this lady came walking by. The trail passes right through this river via the large rocks I was laying on. This lady was a welcomed sight. She sat down with me and started talking. She said she was on her way back to Kalalau and asked me where I was going. I explained to her that I had decided to go back because of my feet and hadn't planned on the hike to be quite like it was. I also explained to her that I had been fasting and was having a hard time.

She agreed with my decision. She also offered me some food so that I could get my energy up for the return hike. I accepted her trail mix and dried fruit for the hike and thanked her. She said she would see me later, once I made it to

73

*Kalalau. She got up and said she needed to go, as she wanted to get there before dark. I asked her about the rest of the trail and she said it was another six miles with a few hard hills, but was much the same as I had already done. I decided to rest for the remainder of the afternoon and to start back early in the morning. I learned a lot from this first trip along the Napali Coast. I got to know exactly what was necessary to take along and what was extra junk that added unnecessary weight. Also, I learned not to start a fast and expect my body to perform hard work. I opened a new chapter in my book of trust and faith in myself, and started to understand my inner voice. I had a lot of time, while walking the trail, to reflect on myself and my life. It was a very peaceful experience; walking the trail was a meditation to me.*

*One has to be extremely alert while walking on this path, as there are places where the trail is only a few feet wide, and then it drops off a cliff hundreds of feet, straight down into the ocean below. It was a long hike out, a total of eight miles from the second valley to the beginning of the trail, and then it took awhile to get a ride back into camp.*

*By the time I got back to the campsite, I was pretty exhausted, but I needed to set up camp again for the night. I got settled and talked to a few other campers about the infection on my feet. I had to boil some water and clean my cuts. I was able to get some ointment that was good for the staff infection, and one of the campers gave me some very valuable instructions on the care for this kind of infection. One of the main things was to keep the cuts covered. Once my feet were healed, I was ready to try the hike again to Kalalau.*

I began my journey much the same as before. I left early in the morning and headed north to the end of the road. Once again, I put my feet on the Kalalau trail, but this time I ate food for energy and my pack was significantly lighter. Also, I had invested in a pair of reef walkers. (These special kind of Island shoes are fantastic for hiking the trail and thanks to a fellow camper's information, I was truly ready to hike to Kalalau.) Alas, my efforts were rewarded, and I was standing on top of the hill overlooking the Kalalau Valley. The stretch down this red cliff went really fast, as I literally flew the rest of the way. I followed the trail down the hill and came to the river that runs through the valley. I stood there for a few minutes and just watched the water as it moved by. This particular spot is very special to me, as I have spent many hours laying on the rocks and enjoying the river. I then walked across the river and climbed up the hill and walked up onto the heau. I set down the pack I was carrying and just stared at the view. I had a hard time believing what I was seeing. It all looked so familiar to me. The scene I was looking at was exactly what I had just finished painting in a picture before I had left Bellingham. There was the mountain and the beach with the ocean hitting the sand, and the resemblance really blew my mind. I then turned around to look directly in front of me, and there I saw a double rainbow that stretched out over the ocean. As I stood there, it transformed into a triple rainbow, which was something I had never seen before. I found myself unable to stand much longer so I bent down and kneeled on my knees. I was in a state of bliss. Looking out over the ocean at this magnificent triple rainbow, I said out loud to the Universe, "Thank you, God, for bringing me home."

*This moment stands out very clearly in my mind. All of my life I have had dreams and visions of this place, with the mountains in the background, and the ocean nearby, but it wasn't until this moment that I realized I had found the sacred place which I believed to exist somewhere. I have felt an ancient connection with this Island from that moment on. While living in that special valley, I was able to connect with my soul's past and tap into a prior lifetime where I knew I had lived once before. This is how I came to Kauai. This was my beginning.*

*Living on this Island was a major learning experience for me. I stayed in Kalalau Valley for over five months. I started a fast a few days after I arrived and was able to continue for forty days. I met an incredible group of people who I am still in contact with, one of them being Lehshel, the lady I met during my first attempt to reach the valley. She was the person who gave me the food so I could get back to town. They were my family, and gave me the acceptance I had never found in the world. They allowed me the space to soar and experience my own highs. They didn't try to hold me back. They watched me transform my being to become one with my higher self, and they gave me support and encouragement. In this sacred Valley of Kalalau (the valley of the healing light), I was able to understand the path that was before me. Most of all, I was able to place my feet upon it.*

*The time I spent in Kalalau was one of the most incredible aspects of my entire life. It gave me the opportunity to get to know the Island of Kauai. There, I spent a lot of time listening and becoming one with the earth. It was here that I heard the Island speak. There was a doorway presented, and I was able to walk through it. My solitary walk to Kalalu was my initiation. My offerings were my fast and my sincerity to become one with myself.*

*I remember so clearly the day that I was sitting on a rock in the middle of the river, listening to the water flow down to become one with the ocean; I felt a change come over me. I had a vision of myself coming forward and merging with a light being. It was at that moment that I felt whole within; I felt complete. The time in Kalalau was instrumental in opening the doorway for my light work on the planet.*

*Until one can understand themselves and become one with themselves, it is difficult to be able to reach out to mankind with anything to offer. Kauai itself is a spiritual vortex. It is a very remarkable place. Living so close to the earth during my first stay there was very special to me. I know that this was the reason I have always had such a close connection with the Island. I got to know a lot about her. (Kauai definitely has a feminine disposition.)*

*It was revealed to me many years later from my first connection in Kalalau that Kauai is Lemuria. It is actually the remaining mountaintops of an ancient continent once known as Lemuria. This fact has been revealed to me many times over. There was a period of time when I didn't talk about it, but then I kept having these incredible connections with visitors from all over the world who gave me the same information. I found it very interesting to be hearing this from people I had never met. We all had a lot of insight in common about Lemuria, and the more this kept occurring, the better I felt about talking about it. Some of the things we have all experienced were the dreams and visions of the scenery on Kauai. I had never been to Kauai before, nor had I ever seen any pictures of it. I found it hard to believe the numbers of folks who have ended up on Kauai much like I had, from a calling or an uncontrollable urge to go there. Once we got there, it all felt and looked so familiar. How do you explain this to someone? I still can't explain it; I can only tell you what occurred. It is very astonishing to me that so many people I have met while living on the Island have experienced a very similar situation to mine.*

*I know that Kauai is a very ancient place. I have heard her call my name, and I believe in my heart and soul that I have, indeed, lived there during another time when the place was known as Lemuria. I know that is why, once again, I was able to find this Island. The experiences I have had over the last fifteen years are very precious to me, and Kauai will always be my soul's eternal home. I feel at one with her when I am there. And when I'm far away, I have the ability to travel there in my mind and rest on her sacred ground. Kauai has been a teacher for me and has given me so much. I know that the tests and lessons sometimes have taken me to the core of my being, but always I come away stronger and clearer. I know she has opened herself to me and embraced me, as I always feel loved and welcomed when my feet touch her ground. I can say that she is a hard teacher and makes many demands of her students, but if you can pass her tests, your life will be richer and hold a deeper meaning for you. I will never forget the first time I heard Kauai speak, calling my name, and I know that each time she calls to me, I will listen with great respect and I will answer.*

Chapter Five

# Introduction to Crystal Healing

Let us return to the natural gifts from the Earth Mother
and receive Healing for all humanity.

I'd like to share with you a form of healing that has much
to offer. Presently, there is very little information available on
the art of crystal healing, and I'm hoping that this chapter will
allow people to better understand the wondrous mineral
kingdom, and the healing it holds for us.

The art of crystal healing and healing with gems is
definitely a part of our past. Many other cultures have kept
alive the use of gems for healing. Our culture is just now
awakening to the use of gems for healing. I feel this is partly
due to the lack of trust people have in the current medical
doctors and forms of treatment available. Up until now, crystal
healing was something that was chosen only as a last resort,
with little hope of any real success. As more and more people
come away with a positive experience, it helps pave the way
for the others to try. I have recently seen a lot more people
come to crystal healing with an open mind, and not as a last
resort.

I first began working with crystals in 1980. At that time,
I was involved in the healing arts as a massage therapist. I
incorporated crystals into the work I was doing. Gradually,
I grew more and more involved with crystals and gem therapy
and let go of the massage. I found there was an ample supply

*of people available for massage, but that very few had opened up to the minerals on the levels that I had. My sincere love and interest in the mineral kingdom has been my vehicle for success with crystal healing.*

*I'd like to share with you what one can expect to experience in a crystal healing, what one should look for in seeking out a person to do crystal healing, and what levels of healing one receives from the mineral kingdom. I am writing this information based on my own personal experience as a crystal healer, and the sessions I have participated in over the last ten years while working with crystals and gems for healing. I stress crystals and gems because the mineral kingdom is vast, and each and every gem and mineral has its own personal gift on a healing basis.*

*It is the ability to learn from the gems and work on their level that allows for healing results. One can obtain the best understanding of the gems by personal experience. There are many books available which seem contradictory as to the healing properties of each gemstone. That is because each person has a different experience with each gem. It is true that gems and their healing abilities fall into certain categories, but I feel that too much emphasis has been placed on what each stone does, and not enough on the personal experiences with the gems themselves. I'd also like to say that so much depends on the person that is working with the stones, i.e. their ability to tune into the stones and their level of developed intuition and trust. I can't emphasize enough that the stones work closely with the person using them. They work within our belief structure which is not to say that they depend upon our beliefs to work, but that the less we limit them with our beliefs, the more they can assist us. Therefore,* when I set out to remove pain from someone, I think unlimited thoughts. I believe what I am doing is possible. I find that the crystals work exceptionally well when I don't limit what they can do with my thoughts.

I stress over and over that the gems and crystals are only tools, that they simply assist us and fine-tune our own healing abilities. Like all tools, they help us perfect and perform our jobs better. When a participant is open to receiving the healing, it only helps to achieve better results.

What can one expect to receive from a crystal and gem healing session? A lot of what you receive depends on how you participate in the session. I require that a person be open to receive healing, and to take responsibility for their healing. I feel very strongly that we create our own illness, and must take responsibility for the creation of wellness. Therefore, when someone comes to me for a session, I stress the importance of realizing that I am only a channel for healing, and that the true healing comes from within themselves, and that it is due to a combined effort that we accomplish anything. Once a person is ready to accept responsibility for themselves, I find that my work is very easy. So often in the regular medical society, people are constantly giving their personal power to the doctor, saying, "I'm sick, doctor, so you make me well." This leaves no responsibility with the individual, and takes the matter out of their hands. I find that working with people who have a desire to heal themselves is very fulfilling. I work very much with the individual, and together we create the results. I will concentrate on the gems and crystals I am using while the person I am working with will be activating their visual abilities and their subconscious mind. While working with visual suggestions and breathing

81

*techniques, I am able to work within the person's aura field. It is impossible to work on a person with crystals and not penetrate their aura. I actually move it, and go through it to the deeper levels of the individual. A lot of the work I have seen over the last few years has centered in on the chakras, or energy centers of the body. I find that the major blocks lie within self-denial and the inability to truly accept and unconditionally love oneself. I address this issue gently, first balancing the appropriate chakra. If the issue centers around a lack of self-love, I will use a lot of rose quartz and rhodochrosite. Once I feel a return of balance, I will move onto the next block. I find that a majority of people are blocked in the heart chakra and the solar plexus. Once we restore harmony, I can assist on other levels of healing.*

*I had worked with a person who had cancer, an older woman. She was very open to what we were doing. I found a great deal of anger and self-denial buried within her energy centers. We worked a lot on self-love and acceptance. I also found her throat chakra completely blocked. I worked to clear that block and to encourage her to change her past habit of not speaking her true feelings. She was amazed at the level of awareness I was able to demonstrate in working with her. Most people don't realize that for someone like myself, the intuitive process is no different than reading a book. Granted, the words are written in a different form, but once one develops the ability to understand the language, it's only a matter of reading the written messages. Our session was very successful. I later received a letter of appreciation from her for the work I had done. She showed amazing results after just one session. For most people, one session is all that I do.*

*If a person will remain sensitive to and aware of what*

brought them to me in the first place, and take care not to perpetuate the problem, the results are lasting. Again, I work to restore balance in their power spots (chakras), to restore their energy, and to clear and mend their auric field. I have seen that once I have restored balance to the chakras and cleared the blocks, the way is opened for their own personal healing, allowing them to heal themselves. There are no limits to what kinds of healings one can receive. I have worked with people on all levels of healing including physical, mental, emotional, and psychic.

Most sessions begin with a gem layout, where I can read the energy centers and restore balance. I have, however, done a lot of sessions focused on specific problems such as a ten-year case of migraine headaches, a back injury, tumors, a pain in different areas, etc. Because I find such a direct connection between the current problems and the emotional condition of the individual, I work a lot on that level. In the sessions, I also make available Bach flower essences and gem elixirs. I also do hands-on healing where I will work with my bare hands to conduct an energy flow that radiates heat to an injured area or sick organ. I have never had a person come for a crystal healing and not receive positive results.

I have a great deal of faith in the healing power of the individual, and I feel that all I am doing is assisting the person in getting in touch with their own healing power. Because the gems and crystals are such a gentle, non-threatening way to heal, I have experienced only good outcomes from working with them. I know that in the next ten-year period we will be seeing a great increase of people turning to the mineral kingdom for healing. Because it addresses the root of the illness and leaves no dangerous *side effects, people can receive this kind of help and not be afraid of the outcome.*

*Over the years, I have acquired a wonderful collection of healing gems that I use strictly for my healing layouts. Little by little, the collection has grown to include tools that are very special and very powerful in the healing realms. I feel honored to be entrusted with such a great responsibility, as to work with these tools demands respect. I have learned that the clearer I become in my work and the more I evolve and grow in my ability to trust and be sensitive, the more the level of tools grows with me. This is something that takes time. I find that the level at which my work exists today is greatly advanced from that of the first session I did years ago. Each session builds strength, adds trust, and develops faith. I feel it is important when one is looking to receive a crystal healing that they seek out a healer that has developed a good rapport with the mineral kingdom. The length of time is not the only aspect one needs to examine.*

*I know souls today who are highly evolved, who possess within their memories vast knowledge and are very capable crystal workers, even though they have only been practicing for several months. There are only a handful of folks working with the stones for healing, and the people I have worked with have had a lot of the same experiences I have had. The information being recalled is from another lifetime, where we excelled in the crystal work. I feel very certain that when a person is seeking to receive a crystal healing, they will attract the healer that is right for them. It is important to go with your intuitive feelings. Talk with the healer and find out about their experiences working with gems, and their background. Be clear with the healer regarding what they are asking for on a financial basis, or what your exchange will be. I feel very strongly that the financial part should not stand in the way of the healing and the work that is to take place. If it doesn't feel right, don't get involved. I've discovered that those who are truly administering their gifts will have reached a balance in their fees, and will work with people so that each individual will receive what they need.*

*I have personally trained individuals who seek me out to learn more about the art of crystal healing. I'm very devoted to teaching, as I see there is a growing need for more people who can assist others with this art. A love for the mineral kingdom and the true desire to help are really all that a person needs to be able to learn. I find that people learn very quickly once they open to the level of the stones and begin to receive from them. The rest is just a matter of practice and building confidence.*

*The actual crystal layout is, of course, very different for each person. There are no two sessions at all alike. The sessions last for approximately one hour. A person usually is laying down. It is very relaxing, non-stressful, and doesn't hurt on a physical level. The person is conscious at all times, and is aware of what is happening. Gems are placed on their body, but very little physical contact is made. The gems I use to place on the energy centers consist of a simple set of seven chakra stones. Starting with the first chakra and continuing onto the seventh, I use obsidian, carnelian, tiger's eye, rose quartz, blue lace agate, amethyst and finally, clear quartz. From this basic seven, I will elaborate as needed. I often place the person in a grid-a formation of crystals around the individual-and work to repair the aura and increase the energy field. I usually approach each session with a focus on either an emotional or a physical healing, dealing with the issues of greatest need. To elaborate a bit more, say that a person comes for help with a migraine headache. This situation calls for a focusing upon a specific physical condition, and I will direct my energies with this focus in mind. Although I use some of the same general techniques in both types of healing, the process is a bit different for physical healing than it is for emotional balancing.*

*Once the basic layout is complete, I spend whatever time is needed in order to close down the areas I have opened up. There are several different techniques that work for this. Passing a crystal back and forth over the person's body will close down the energy. I often work with feathers to brush over the aura and balance the energy. This part of the session is extremely important because when crystals are directed at the individual, they penetrate the aura and into their physical being. The practice of re-sealing the aura and bringing the person into a comfortable extension of their energy field is critical. Once the session is completed, the person will be aware of different vibrational changes, subtle, yet very noticeable. Lastly, I will use Bach flower essences and gem elixirs for additional help in specific areas of healing, both emotional and physical. These aid the person with on-going healing.*

*I hope that this introduction has given you a little better understanding of what crystal healing can offer. If you feel drawn to crystals and gems for healing, I encourage you to seek out an individual who can assist you. There are only a few of us who are currently offering this form of healing, but if you are sincere, you will attract the one that will help you.*

*In the following chapters, I go into more detail about crystal healing. I write about actual healing sessions I have given, and then share a few personal testimonies from individuals who have experienced working with me during a crystal healing session.*

Chapter Six

# The Healing Sessions

*The beauty of being a part of healing is felt completely in my soul.*

*As a child of twelve years old, I realized I had a gift. At that time, it came through my hands with their natural ability to generate heat. Now, many years later, I have been able to incorporate this gift into   something I can offer to others.*

*My healing work using crystals and other gemstones has fulfilled a desire in me to help others in the area of healing. Realizing my natural abilities, I feel that working with crystals amplifies the healing one receives. As for myself, I have studied many forms of healing, and now that I am working with the stones, I feel satisfied that I have found my medium in the healing arts, and I feel complete working with them.*

*I would like to share with you a few of the crystal healings I have participated in over the years. Each healing is unique unto the person. No one healing is greater or better than another; however, there are always those experiences that stand out in your mind. I have been involved in using crystals for healing for ten years now. Over this period, I have always been amazed at the folks who find me. I have never done any extensive advertising or attempted to attract business, so to speak. I have relied on the Universe to bring me the people who I can assist. Together, we share a positive experience while working. Over the years, I have participated in several* hundred healings.  I am sharing only a few of these experiences with you, ones that I trust will give you a better understanding of the vast range that is covered while working with the mineral kingdom.  There are no limitations, only those that we impose on ourselves. During the sessions using the stones for healing, I have been given a clear understanding of the unique uses and properties of certain gems.  One starts to see a pattern while working with the crystals.  I work very closely with the healing stones that I have acquired, and have come to know intuitively which ones can best assist me for a particular need.  I feel my success comes through my ability to become one with the gems and work with them on their level.  Each account shared here is taken from an actual crystal healing session with the person mentioned. Certain individuals prefer to remain anonymous. Therefore, I chose not to use a name rather than pick out a fictitious one. The following information is given to each person who comes for a crystal healing session. I was given this format to share via my guides at thre o'clock a.m. one morning, five years ago in 1985 on Kauai.)

The following flyer is all that I give to anyone to explain what I do in a crystal healing session:

89

# HEALING HANDS

*The ability to release old emotional blocks with the assistance of gems through chakra balancing is a very powerful form of healing.*

Our lives, our Beings are an expression of our emotions. Before we can truly love and experience joy, it is essential that the blocks be removed.

Our own self-denial and inability to truly accept and unconditionally love ourselves is our first major block. Working together, we are able to heal this block, receive forgiveness, and be able to forgive. Through this, we learn to love our self and all of ourselves, unconditionally. And in turn, we can offer this form of love, this inner peace to others, our family and our World.

The first step is critical as before we can move on, we must clear the blocks.

The sessions consist of a combination of flower remedies and chakra balancing with the use of crystals and gemstones. Each session requires the openness of the individual and the recognition of combined cooperation toward the goal of personal healing.

I have been working with the ancient art of Gem Therapy over a period of ten years. I have experienced time and time again very wonderful healings through the ability to release the emotional blocks and restore balance to the chakra's energy centers of the body! I am available to work with anyone who has a sincere willingness and acceptance for creating their own personal healing. Again I emphasize, it is a combined effort — together we accomplish, as all true healing comes from within. I am only here as a Guide.

***GEM THERAPY***
***CHAKRA BALANCING***
***CRYSTAL HEALING***
***GEM ELIXIRS***
***FLOWER REMEDIES***

*I have found this flyer to be an invaluable tool in helping to create and understand what the person is getting into regarding crystal healing. It is very easy to hand this to a person and have them read it. I always ask them if they have any questions. Because we are working in something that is still fairly new as far as the general public is concerned, I feel it is important for them to understand the relationship between myself and them. We are moving rapidly away from the traditional forms of healing, where one goes to see a physician with the mind set of "heal me doctor". It is important to set the stage from the very beginning so that a person doesn't start to think in old patterns. One thing I have to attest to regarding the high rate of success in the crystal healing sessions is that I make it clear from the beginning that we work together. I am not the healer and you are not the patient. Once a person comes to me, I know they have decided that they are ready to change. This self-chosen prerequisite really sets it all up from the beginning. I know that by working with divine guidance, the folks who find me and appear for a healing are truly ready to break free from what they have created, and move on to a higher level of personal peace. I learned the hard way that I can't give anything to anyone unless they first ask for it, and truly want to receive it. Once I had this understanding, I realized that I couldn't help everyone, and that I had to wait and be ready to receive only the individuals who were destined to work with me. This one revelation has given me endless peace. I see over and over again the Universe setting up the most incredible cosmic connections for the folks I am meant to work with. People have appeared at my front door with no other means of contact other than through divine guidance. It's not like you can open*

*the yellow pages in a phone book and find me. I work on an
entirely different level of connection. A friend of a friend will
mention my name, and the person will have this calling to
meet with me. I have experienced numerous ways in which
the Universe has set up these meetings, and each one is
perfect. I remain open to receive and focus a lot on light
energy, connecting with individuals who can cooperate for the
higher purpose we strive to create.*

## Dena Walker

It was during my second visit to Oahu that I was given
the opportunity to assist Dena in her personal
transformation. I was on Oahu to give a crystal workshop
and offer healing sessions.  Once again, I was staying with
Dena at her house in Manoa Valley.  She is one of the ladies
I work with when I go to Oahu.  She helped set up the
workshop, and assisted me while I was there.  I had been
busy with sessions and was aware that Dena was waiting
her turn.  There was a point, after a very long day of working
one session after another from early morning until the late
hours of night, when I knew she was wondering if I was
going to have time to work with her.  I looked at her very
directly and said, "Don't worry, I won't forget you."  It was
early the following morning when I announced to her, "Okay,
Dena, I'm all yours."  I had been doing the healing work in
her room.  There was an incredible energy present, as the
room was literally filled with light.

I had been kidding with Dena all along, since the first time
that I had met her, about the fact that I knew who she was
and she wasn't fooling me with her attempt to hide out. I
also told her to be ready for some really obvious changes, as
once we did our work there would be no turning back.

The session with Dena was very different from any healing

I have yet to encounter. One needs to understand the format of the session, and then they will be able to relate to what occurred. I will share what unfolded, and then describe it as it happened. The session began like this: We began as usual with an offering of gratitude and surrounded ourselves with light, asking for assistance from our guides, angels, and other healing energies that were in harmony with our work. I placed certain stones on the chakra centers that needed balancing. On her solar plexus, I placed the largest citrine crystal I had. We then began the session. It occurred solely as a guided visualization, where I suggested certain images and she followed. We ended up going on an incredible journey where a lot was revealed through images and events.

Please note that nothing was planned, as the whole session and the method I used were completely spontaneous. I worked a long time on her aura, removing the unwanted energies and sealing up the holes that were there. Once I had restored the aura and increased the energy there, I sat down at her feet. We began with opening her crown chakra and bringing in light. I asked Dena to go in her mind to a place somewhere that was outside, a place that was special to her, one that gave her comfort and peace. I then suggested that she find a path and begin walking on it. I asked her to look around and appreciate the beauty all around her. As she walked the path, I continued to move the light through her body, assisting her with gentle breathing and telling her she would find herself climbing higher and higher on the path until at last she found herself high atop a mountain. I assisted her in walking to the edge of the cliff and looking down at the valley below her. Then I told her to look up and see the bird above her. I asked her to become one with the bird.

At this point things really began to move. I spoke gently, and guided Dena in flight. I watched her in my mind as she flew. I guided her to soar, to feel the wind in her wings. I whispered, "Dena, catch the current. You are free to soar higher, higher." She travelled, and then she was above the valley. I asked her to plant her seed in the valley, to let it grow-her seed of truth, of healing-her gift would grow. I guided her on flying over the valley. The seed grew into a tree, and it blossomed, and seeds fell, and the trees multiplied, and as she flew, her seeds travelled. They grew until the valley was a mass. We travelled together, me as her guide. I saw her gliding and soaring over an incredible valley of trees that had grown from the seed she had planted. I realized at this point the importance of her work. I knew she would reach many heights, and would be an incredible tool for the healing and transformation work that was in motion on the planet. I was guiding her over the valley of trees and guiding her to see the trees, to notice the bountiful forest that had grown from her seeds. I asked her to see the beauty and acknowledge what she had planted. At that point in the healing, the energy was very high. I was vibrating all over, and my body began to cry with joy. I took a deep breath and grabbed for composure. Meanwhile, Dena was flying. She was really out there. At this juncture, I focused on her flight. I felt for a split second that Dena was going to completely transcend the earth plane and keep going. It was at this moment that I gently, but firmly took control. I said "Dena, soar gently downward, closer and closer. Now you will see the mountaintops below you. Gently glide toward the mountain ever so slowly, down...down. Feel the earth on your feet, let your wings embrace the wind as you touch the land, gently. Become one again with your body, feel your feet on the trail, and begin the descent down the mountain. The valley of your seed is around you. Enjoy the beauty and serenity of your creation." I guided her slowly to walk down the path before her. I suggested a flowing river. I asked her to embrace the water and flow with the river. We travelled down the river, me in my mind watching and guiding her onward toward the sea. Finally, we arrived at the river's edge and we joined the ocean. I asked her to see the ocean and to feel its power. "Listen to the waves as they touch the sand," I said. "Swim and feel the turquoise water all around you." I guided her at last to the sand, and asked her to walk onto the beach. I asked her to feel the earth under her feet. I was working hard at this point to ground Dena back to the earth plane, because she had gone completely out of her body, and she was very difficult to bring back. I use several different techniques to ground a person. I did them all with Dena. I sealed her aura by running a crystal over her energy field. I used my owl feathers to brush her aura. I used my hands to gently brush her body. Still, Dena's energy was hitting the ceiling of the room. I then resorted to my last technique, where I go to a person's feet, pick them up, and gently drop them. This always works. I then tested her energy level and found it to be at a comfortable place, about five feet above her body. Shutting a person down is very important. You can't send someone back out on the streets of Oahu with their energy field out in space. I told Dena that I was going to leave for just a moment to wash my hands. I always do this as soon as I have the person grounded, as I want to disperse the energy as quickly as possible. Whenever I do healing work, I have learned to keep the energy in my hands and arms, never allowing it to go past my elbows. At times my hands become very sore, but once I wash them off and give the energy back to the Universe in the form of white light, the energy is recycled and restored to balance. I have never had any problem with taking on anyone's energy since I learned this technique. A woman healer that I studied with taught me how to contain the energy, and explained how to use cold, running water to completely release the energy. I am eternally grateful for her guidance in this area. There are healings that drain my energy because they are very intense, but I am tired for only one day, and then I'm fine.

After I had washed my hands and completely released the energy, I walked back to the door and very slowly walked in.

The light in the room was very bright, and Dena was still laying there on the floor. I walked over and sat down beside her. At this point, I was completely high from the healing. I was amazed at the whole experience. I assisted Dena in sitting up and looked into her eyes. For a moment, I was unable to speak. In fact, I don't think either of us spoke at all for quite a while. I remember getting it together to go and do some other work. A lady came to pick me up, as she wanted me to do an energy-clearing on her house and to meet with her husband to do a crystal healing. I made arrangements with Dena to meet her later. We were going to have dinner together. It wasn't until later that evening after dinner while we were driving in the car before Dena and I spoke about what had transpired during the session. I asked Dena how the session was for her, and made the comment that it was a most extraordinary experience for me. She shared a little with me, and at first it was hard to talk about. We did get around to the part where she was flying. I shared with her how at that point I felt I was going to lose her. I told her I had been crying with joy, and at the same time working to take control. She commented that she was really glad that I told her to see the mountaintop, and that at that particular point she had to make a conscious choice to come back. We didn't talk very much, as I knew the whole experience had really blown both of our minds. The session did create an invincible bond between Dena and myself, and still to this day our connection is very strong. I hear her call my name when she needs my help, and I have found her to be there just the same for me. Her strength and power are now in full force, and the work she is doing is truly one of planting seeds of truth. Her forest has literally grown over a large area. I go often to Dena's valley and just hang out there in my mind. The vision and journey we took that day will remain sacred to me, always.

# A Friend from Kauai

In this recollection of a crystal healing, we are journeying back to my very first experience using stones for healing. I would like to go back to the beginning and share with you how this area of healing opened up for me, and what events shaped the outcome of my work. At this time, I was living on the northernmost point of the Island of Kauai (Haena). In the Hawaiian language, it means "the end of the road". I lived in a house near the water, where there was a beautiful beach. I had been doing my massage work in my home, as my son was only a year old, and I was responsible for our support. While my son napped, I used the time to do healing work. In my back yard I had a hot tub, and I would place my clients in the tub first, and then do a massage. This combination was really powerful, because it allowed me to remove tension that I wasn't ordinarily able to address. Living on Kauai is an experience in itself. This Island is a very powerful spot. I credit a lot of my growth to the fact that I lived there for so long. Living on Kauai, I feel a person is given an initiation into the ancient ways. It was while living on Kauai that I was introduced to the ancient path of the Kahunas by way of Huna. Huna is the philosophy of the Hawaiians, and it is a way of life based on ancient truths, rather than a religion. For me, simply living there was my first teacher, learning to understand spirit and nature and the ancient ways. For me, learning came firsthand from the Island and the extraordinary experiences that I encountered on a daily basis. It was during this period that I was given the realization of my path-the rainbow warrior. I received my amakuas (totems), the owl and dolphin; I found out who I was and got to meet my soul face to face. I'm always telling folks that living on Kauai is not like living in Minneapolis. I say this kiddingly, but in my heart I'm really trying to get a point across, with no disrespect meant to the citizens of Minneapolis. Kauai is a very unique place to live. The

Island is a very powerful teacher, and one learns great respect once they get to know her. During this time on the north shore, I felt my learning was somewhat of a crash course. I was having some amazing dreams and visions, and it all was leading up to my rediscovery of crystals. I kept having this one dream where I was with a group of people going for a hike, and everyone was leaving me behind. I then discovered a cave and found a box. I opened the box, and inside there were a few crystal tools and various other rocks. (It wasn't until I had been given my first crystal that I was able to identify the tools in the dream as crystals.) Then, once I had uncovered these tools, an old man appeared and said, "You have discovered the ancient secrets, the stones that hold the key for healing mankind. Because you have found them, it is meant for them to go with you." I started to argue with the man, exclaiming that I wasn't ready, and that I didn't know how to use them. All of a sudden the man vanished, and in the distance I heard his voice chanting, "Key for mankind, key for mankind." This dream was such a regular with me that it has always remained clearly in my mind. The other event that was very major for me at this time was seeing the movie Superman. I didn't own a T.V. and at the time I had no car. So when I did see a movie, this was pretty rare. However, I did get to see the original Superman movie. This movie again said a lot to me. When Superman found the crystal and travelled to the crystal room, it felt so familiar to my being. I'm sharing all of this because it was a very definite part of the unfolding for me. Very shortly after all of this, I was given my first clear quartz crystal. This particular crystal is very different than any one I have ever seen. I still have this crystal, and continue to use it during my healing sessions. The following account is about the first time I used this crystal for healing. I had been doing massage for a friend of mine who had been in a car accident years before. After the accident, she was given surgery on her knee. The surgery left her leg stiff and unable to bend at the knee. She was told this was from the scar tissue that formed after the operation. The fact that she was not able to bend this leg at all added to the stress on her entire body. Up to this point, I had been working on her twice a week. She would soak in the hot tub and then receive a massage. This session started out much the same as all the others. I had her soak for awhile in the tub, and then I began her massage. I worked on her shoulder and neck areas, as she carried a lot of pain in these areas. When I arrived at her knee, I first rubbed the area and did my usual work to remove the tension. Then I flashed on the new crystal I had been given. I asked my friend if she was willing to let me try something new. I explained to her that I was going to work with this crystal, and see if I could remove some of the pain and tension. She had no objections, so I began. I took the crystal in my right hand and held it directly over the wounded knee area. I then began circling it very slowly in a clockwise direction. After I circled, I would draw the crystal slowly up and pull out the energy. I was working solely on my inner guidance, as this was the first time in this lifetime I had used a crystal in this manner. It seemed really natural and very easy for me to do. But then, as I continued to circle the crystal and draw out the energy, something very strange occurred. There was an obvious popping sound that we both heard, very loud and clear. Mind you, I wasn't even touching the area. I was simply passing the crystal over the knee and drawing the energy up and out. My friend sat up and looked at me. We were both in shock, as the noise sounded like one had cracked their neck or something, like when you go to the chiropractor. I finished with rubbing the leg and continued pulling the energy out with my hands. It was really interesting when I was working with the crystal, as I could feel the tension breaking up each time I passed it over the knee. After I finished the session, my friend sat up on the edge of the table, and I went to assist her in getting down. While she was sitting on the edge with her one leg hanging down, she started to bend her other knee. As I held her, she got very excited. "Almitra", she yelled. "I can bend my knee!" I got a hold of her and helped lift her to the ground, and sure enough, she could now bend the knee at an angle. She was not able to bend it completely in half. However, she could bend it slightly, enough to make a great impression on the two of us. I was amazed. When she had arrived, her leg was completely stiff, unable to bend at all. Now here she stood before me walking, and as she did, her left knee was able to bend slightly, to make the movement much less stressful. I didn't know what to say. I remember commenting on the loud pop, and that somehow the crystal had been successful in breaking up the scar tissue and giving her some slack. I continued working on her as usual during our massage sessions; however, this session was definitely a turning point in my life and instrumental in opening the door for my healing work with crystals. It's been ten years since I did this first session with my friend on the north shore of Kauai. I have seen so many wonderful healings since then that I could easily write a book just about that.

## Elizabeth West

Elizabeth appeared at my door one day with the assistance of a couple of friends of mine. The second my eyes embraced this woman I felt an ancient connection with her. Elizabeth was in a very difficult time in her life and had come to see me with the intention of making some changes. Immediately I saw through the temporary cloud of confusion of her higher self and got a glimpse of a truly magnificent being. I knew that the light energy I saw in her at that time in her life was not recognizable to her. She was consumed in a very dark depression and confusion about the very question of her existence. I felt an immediate strong love energy for this woman and my heart opened directly on the spot to assist her. We left the others that had brought her up to see me and went into the crystal healing room. I worked with Elizabeth to do an invocation of the light and offered a prayer for her to the Universe (God). I then began my work with her to remove the blocks and pockets of pain that were so present in her heart and solar plexus. Elizabeth was in terrible pain and sadness; she cried through most of the session. I knew she was hoping for an immediate healing. I spoke with her once the session was completed. I made her a combination of flower remedies and gem essences. I promised her that she would feel things lifting within three to four weeks, and that we had done a lot of work today to get things moving out. I also explained to her that these things take time. One doesn't heal a lifetime of trauma in one hour. I told her that I needed to see her once more in about a month. I knew that things were going to change for her rapidly, but I felt a loss in reassuring her. I spoke with Elizabeth a few days later, as I could feel her releasing even though I was several hundred miles away. I called to see how she was doing. I continued to work with Elizabeth from a distance and still today she isn't aware of the hours I have spent in communion with her higher self from a distance with the focus of removing sorrow. It was the second crystal healing session that Elizabeth and I shared almost two months later that was the turning point for both of us. Elizabeth came this time to see me by herself. The energy was extremely high. There was a lot going on in her life and I wanted so much to help her make a breakthrough. We entered the healing room once again to address her issues. However, this time it was very powerful. I received an incredible understanding about our connection and know that I was able to see Elizabeth truly in harmony with her higher self, united, free from pain, and shining in the true sense of the light being she is. Elizabeth's commitment to moving through the blocks was felt in every cell of my being. Never had I seen a person come with such devotion to healing themselves. There was a point in the middle of the session when I was guiding Elizabeth in visualizing golden light moving through her crown chakra and out her solar plexus, when the energy was vibrating so strongly that I was shaking intensely. I had to stop and leave the room for a minute. This was a first for me. When I walked back into the dome, there lay Elizabeth before me on a shimmering altar of light that was so magnificent I started to cry. There before me I saw a high priestess, a goddess of love and light, and it touched me deeply. I resumed my work with a new understanding, a calling from deep within my soul to assist this angel to be all that I knew she was. We completed this session and I know it has affected both of our lives in a very powerful way. The changes in Elizabeth are unbelievable; she had been able to transcend all of her blocks, and her life is unfolding in the most amazing way.

This woman has an incredible capacity for love and healing, but it was her inability to love and have confidence in herself that was holding her back. I'm truly grateful to be of service to individuals like Elizabeth. It was her desire to break free combined with my ability to remove blocks, that gave us this dynamic experience. I know that our connection is eternal, and I feel blessed having her back in my life once again. I know that she has incredible gifts to offer humanity, and she will be doing so in the very near future.

## Hal Booth

Hal is a person I have known for three years. It was while we were working together marketing some health care products that his wife, Nancy, informed me that Hal was scheduled for heart surgery in one week. I felt an immediate concern for Hal. I knew that at his age another surgery would be a great risk, and I feared for his life literally. I decided I would ask him if he was open to an alternative to surgery. I simply asked him, "Hal, would you consider trying something else to remove the block in your heart?" Hal knew a little about the work I do but I had never gone into any detail about the specifics of my healing methods. I explained to him that if he was open to working with me, I felt certain that we could remove the block and avoid surgery. I know that because I have been friends with Hal for years, there is a certain level of trust between us. He agreed it was worth a try, and I made arrangements with Nancy to establish a time we could meet at the office in town for a session. I met with Hal one week later, three days before he was scheduled for his surgery.

The healing with Hal began much like other sessions. Nancy wanted to be present for the healing. I explained to her the importance of focusing her thoughts on the goal of the session. I told her if she felt she could stay centered with us she was welcome to be there. As I started the session with Hal, the first thing I did was to have a talk with myself. I focused my mind on the healing we were about to preform, I set aside my ego, and let go of any limitations in my thoughts. I reminded myself that this issue was not any different from any other and that there are no limits to healing. At first I felt a little apprehensive, and somewhat pressured as on one level a blocked artery in the heart is a serious issue. As I centered and opened up the channel for divine order and focused on the love I felt for Hal and Nancy, I was ready to start. I did my usual prayer surrounding all of us with the purest form of white light available. I guided Hal in breathing in some different colors. I worked with pink light in the beginning to bring in peaceful energies. Then I explained to Hal that I was going to work with a laser wand and with his help on focusing to remove the block, I would work with the crystal. Hal was guided to focus on his heart and in his mind he was to see the block being removed. I asked him to let me know when he had gotten the visual image, and that I would count to three. I listened for his cue and began counting very slowly, one...two... three... and on the count of three, I had pulsed the laser to remove the block at the same time he was focusing in his mind to remove the block. I then used the laser crystal to pull the energy block out of his heart. I went back into the area with the crystal and pulsed it for healing, and then I used the crystal to put the healing program into his heart area. Once this was accomplished, I worked with the rest of Hal's energy field. He had a lot of stress in his aura that had been accumulated over many years. We ran a lot of color through his body. As he focused on seeing certain colors, I would work with my healing stones to balance and regenerate his being. I felt really positive about the session once it was completed. I tested him for Bach flowers and gave him several gem elixirs to take for follow-up and additional healing assistance. He was also given some green adventurine to wear close to his heart chakra. I advised him to take it easy for at least a full day and did my best to explain that even though he was not given surgery in the traditional form, that it was much the same on a cellular level. I spent almost two hours working with Hal that day, and in my heart I knew that I had given him my best. It wasn't until over a week later that I received a call from Nancy. I had thought about the outcome several times and each time worked with myself to let go of any expectations. When I heard Nancy on the phone I held my breath. She talked about several different things and finally told me that Hal had gone into the hospital and that the block in his heart was completely gone. I was very happy to hear the news and felt a sense of relief come over my being. I credit the success to the fact that Hal was open to receive a healing, and that he trusted me. Had he not been given the opportunity to know me as a friend for the previous years, it is doubtful he would have been willing to try crystal healing. I know that as more and more people can experience the mineral kingdom, it will open the doors for others to try.

*I feel strongly that the gems have so much more to offer us, and as I look back over the years, I realize one thing. When I began, I only had myself and this one stone to listen to. It has been through my devotion to the gems and being able to tune into them on their level, that this work has taken me on my incredible journey. I began ever so simply- trusting and just going forward. Each healing session was a step towards perfection in learning and feeling. My level of intuition has grown, and my healing abilities have accelerated. I feel so blessed as each person I have been able to touch through the crystals and gems has entered upon his own opening to receive, through trusting and believing. I am really grateful to these individuals for giving me the opportunity to work with them. I have witnessed a unique spectrum of individuals coming to me with a variety of needs, and each time I have experienced a healing being given and received. There have been times I have done sessions, one after another, for eight to ten hours at a time. I don't find myself tired. Instead, each time I feel renewed, as if from somewhere there comes an inexhaustible source of strength. I find I am always able to fill my cup and go on. I have noticed over the years that the more I do, the more I understand. I discovered in the first days of doing crystal healing an incredible ability to see into the other person's energy field, almost as if I could see into their body. I could tune in and immediately understand what the problem was, and what they needed. Well, today this ability comes automatically to me, and I find it has become second nature. And along with my level of understanding, I am finding that people are much more open to hearing and receiving guidance on this level. I feel a lot less hesitant to talk to folks about topics such as what gems to use for various results, and how*

105

*to use crystals. I find myself talking openly to strangers. For example, yesterday I was in an office, and the receptionist made a comment on the necklace I was wearing. I explained to her that I made the necklaces, and she asked me if I could make one for her. Then she asked me how much they cost. I told her the price, and I explained to her that it included a reading on what gems would best assist her at this time. I told her my process of talking to her for a few minutes, and then doing a reading of her energy, and then transferring it into stones. I said, "I can't really explain it, but I'm just able to see where you're at and know which gems will help you." She said, "Oh, I understand." I asked her if she had a piece of paper, and then I began the reading. Like I said, it is very simple for me, quite automatic. I just follow my inner guidance and start asking simple questions. I can see what chakras are blocked, and know immediately what stones one needs. I asked the receptionist how her memory was, as I was getting the information that she needed garnets. She said she had a great memory, so I said, "Well then, how's your lower back?" She said it was terrible and I said, "Well then, that answers why you need the garnet!" I continued, and in about ten minutes I had a list of what stones to put in her necklace. She thanked me over and over again and commented on how she could feel the energy from the stones in my own necklace, and how she could basically understand how it works. This is what excites me today. I can offer my gifts openly to people without fear. I find that so much of what I do is on an educational level. I spend a lot of time with people explaining to them what they are receiving, and helping them to learn more about the gems and their individual focuses. I also offer crystals for sale; however, I'm* doing it differently than most individuals selling crystals. I have found that the majority of people now looking to purchase crystals are doing so because they are interested in learning more about their gifts and uses. I have a large variety of gems and crystals, and I offer them to folks by appointment. That way, I can work with the person on a one-to-one basis and answer their questions, helping them to understand what they are receiving and how to work with their stones. I have worked a lot in the retail area, but I find that the structure doesn't always allow for the time to share in detail about the properties of the crystals the person is buying. For me, the emphasis lies in serving the customer and the stones. I'm anxious to get the gems to the right person, and I'm committed to giving as much information as I can. For me, selling by appointment is perfect. I am committed to continuing my work through healing and sharing information. I also find a great deal of joy in helping others find their crystals, and have a lot of fun when folks call on me to locate a certain rock. I have experienced time and time again that certain crystals or gems tell me who they are for. Each time I deliver a rock to someone, they are amazed at how I can find the right one. I have mailed crystals all across the country to people who have asked me to locate a certain piece. I'm continually amazed, as I will send the stone, sight unseen to the person, and to this day I have never had anyone return a rock. They are always completely satisfied with the fact that I had indeed located the gem they were looking for. I tell people that it's very simple, because the rocks talk to me. Years ago, I couldn't say this to anyone without getting funny looks. But today, I find a lot of folks agree and understand what I mean when I say, "Rocks talk."

Chapter Seven

# Personal Testimonies

*These are the exact words shared by various individuals who have participated in a crystal healing session with Almitra. They are shared to give one an insight into the experience.*

### Jasmine Leia Whitfield
Age 10

It was nice that Almitra did some crystal work on me. Almitra helped me get rid of my problems, almost like a counselor, but better. At the end of the visit, I felt more strength in me to move around. It seems as though the crystals energize you. It's lots of fun working with Almitra.

### Dena Walker

About three years ago, I had a very profound healing experience with Almitra. This was my second experience with the art of laying on stones, but at this time I was shown the depth this type of subtle body healing could reach. Only a few times have I shared this experience with others, because it has been sacred to me and difficult to capture with words. She began with a prayer, laying some stones on me and beginning a guided visualization. I reached a state of feeling very safe and open with an intention of working very deeply, in total trust with Almitra. I lost sight of my form in the physical body and "took off" into a soaring journey high into the vastness of my potential.

I became a high-flying bird, flying above the ground

(my physical body), moving over places that were familiar and new. It was within this magnificent flight that I could freely let go of blocks on the physical terrain presented. Looking back now, these were areas where I had stored lifetimes of pain or childhood traumas within my heart, throat, or power center regions. My spirit was totally free and felt exhilarated at the expanse now available to it. I continued to soar with the speed of light.

Gently, Almitra kept a strong connection with me, being well aware of how quickly my spirit was moving, and of the intensity at which this healing was hitting. I could see her as a bird flying with me, or trying to catch up with me. From a voice of light, I could hear directions being spoken. One still strong in my mind was,"You are flying above the fertile ground and you are dropping seeds of your dreams." These high aspirations began to grow; within seconds these seeds moved through a lifetime of growth, like speeded up film. The seeds became magnificent orchards of trees, bearing brilliant fruits of light. There was a point where my spirit took the lead and needed to be redirected to land. Almitra guided me back to my body. When I got back to my physical body, I could see how much had shifted within myself, and how new everything was, and how I would no longer be the same. She had focused on my solar plexus with a citrine, my throat chakra with an aqua, and my heart with rose quartz. These regions were pulsing with new life and an openness. This moment lasted really only a few minutes, but felt eternal. I got glimpses of what had been released out of these energy centers.

Since this crystal healing with Almitra, my life has continued with the exhilarated "pace" the healing moved at. Beautiful changes within my home life, work, and physical body have taken place. That day in Manoa Valley stands out as the day my power center was able to break itself free. It's amazing to me how something so simple could have such a dramatic effect. With earthshaking awareness, I see the power of intention, light, focus, and love.

## In the Light of Almitra's Crystal Dome
## Elizabeth West

When I was given the opportunity to meet Almitra, I knew that Divine Spirit was really watching over me and guiding me. I was in a very weakened, very depressed and confused condition when we met. I was not able to trust my gut level feelings or my own judgment. I also was in a relationship and a job that was not a healthy one for me, and I was in great need of help. I had heard briefly about Almitra and her abilities to facilitate one's healing, both physically and emotionally, through the use of crystals. I immediately wanted to meet with her and an appointment was set up that very week.

The trip to Lummi Island was wonderful. I was enthralled with the beauty of the island and the magnificent place Almitra and her family live. From the moment I laid eyes on Almitra I felt an immediate trust and warmth and knew the decision to meet her and work with her was an important one for me.

We chatted, then relaxed and enjoyed the outdoor hot tub, and then entered her dome where she does her crystal healing work. I had an incredible feeling of being nurtured, loved and cared for. I was completely open with Almitra about who I was and what my concerns were. I felt her loving spirit. She then had me lie on a mattress and she placed a variety of crystals on me from head to toe, while explaining what purpose they served. Then came her amazing process of facilitating the clearing and cleansing of my heart chakra and my crown chakra. They were very blocked. She spoke many beautiful words to me while doing the clearing and I wept continually as she worked. The tears welled up from the depth of my being, coming from the deep

110

pain I have carried for most of my life and at the same time from extreme joy from the release of the pain and blocks.

When she finished this treatment, she worked with a pendulum to determine which gem elixirs and flower essences I needed to further my emotional healing and well-being. I felt so very different when we left the dome. I had a new sense of peace and joy and relief. Almitra explained to me that she did a lot of unblocking work, but that all that I needed could not be accomplished at this one visit and in a month or so she would complete the process. She said I would continue to experience the changes and growth. She was not understating this. I became stronger to deal with my challenging job and relationship and had more clarity and peace.

When I returned a month later, Almitra tuned in to the profound connection we had together. She recognized my deep commitment to healing myself. We then settled ourselves in the dome and Almitra began an intense healing process. She opened a very blocked solar plexus, balancing my power center, cleared my throat chakra, my receiving side, cleared my aura, did a powerful visualization and sent a golden light which filled and surrounded me.

Almitra spent a lot of time on my healing and clearing and at one point had to leave the dome for a few moments because the energy had gotten so intense. She offered me a way to love myself as I never had before. It was a beautiful feeling and an experience I will never forget. The love and caring Almitra puts into her work is unparalleled in my experience. We have a great love for each other and this love continues to deepen. Her work is profound and life changing. As a result of working with Almitra, I have come into my authentic power. I was able to re-connect with my Divine Being. I found the courage and strength to speak my truth and am able to articulate more easily what I want and to create what I want. I was able to not only release a fifteen-year-old job that was hurtful to me, but open myself up enough to draw to me to a new profession I absolutely love. New plans and goals for my life have completely opened up to me. I also have released myself from a suffocating and manipulative relationship. Hurray! I found a peace and joy that up until then I could not contact. My healing continues and I am in profound gratitude to my Divine Being and this blessed spirit named Almitra. I believe in her healing abilities and in her.

## Alexandra Mines

It was through taking one of her crystal workshops that I met Almitra Zion. I'll never forget the evening that we were first introduced. Her eyes seemed to penetrate my soul as she told our group the story about her quest for the Earthkeeper crystal. I noticed that she kept looking over at me. Meanwhile I was experiencing the time-standing-still effect that I always receive when I reconnect with an old soul-friend. By the time Almitra's story was finished, there was not a dry eye, nor an untingling body in the room. In the meantime, the atmosphere had become super-charged with a high vibration of light-energy because of all the crystals among us. I was to experience this energy again and again as the workshop progressed. I was also to experience seeing an aura for the first time. The aura was emanating in a surging wave of eggshell-blue light from one of the group members who was receiving a grid healing at the time. It was more beautiful than words can describe. And amazingly, every single one of us witnessed it. Learning to heal others with gems and crystals is a healing process in and of itself. There is so much to learn, so much to experience, so much to give and receive. I quote Almitra when I say that crystals are a true, wondrous gift to mankind. Furthermore, they are our spiritual companions.

In time, Almitra and I came to realize that our finding each other was no accident. But it was through the healing sessions performed on me that the true extension of our connection was revealed. At the time, I was attempting to break through some emotional blocks that I felt were impeding my spiritual development. Sometimes, the hardest person to love in life is one's self, and I knew that the time had come for me to confront this issue. I was disillusioned with traditional counseling. Oftentimes I find counselors to be more in need of guidance than myself. This may sound pretentious to some, but I have found a good amount of limitedness and witnessed a lot of manipulative ploys on the part of counselors to perpetuate conformity to their own personal belief systems and needs. Does one grow, much less develop trust, in a counseling relationship where outdated paradigms and power roles predominate? I think not. Why waste precious time! In a matter of weeks, utilizing Almitra's gift of healing, the stones, and my own self-healing abilities, we were able to transcend my emotional wounds.

During the sessions, it was quite effortless to travel outside of my body. During one particular session, I traveled to a very beautiful place. I stood on a cliff overlooking a turqouise-blue ocean and sang my power song to the infinite cosmos. I was aware that I was myself, yet I was also someone else. I was reliving a moment from a past life, a very ancient one. All of a sudden, I heard Almitra gasp, and as I returned to my body and opened my eyes the room filled with a brilliant white light, so bright that it was almost blinding. I shut my eyes and went into a dream state. We were encircled by a group of ancient elders who were communicating with Almitra. We were told that night that our friendship spanned the centuries, and that our paths had been reunited in order that we might work together to heal the planet. Furthermore, we discovered that we were related to some of the same ancient ones in the spirit world.

Another time, I was visited by a Hawaiian Kahuna Priest spirit guide, who sang and danced around me, dressed in a floor-length feather cape. When I came back from this journey, it took me several minutes to be able to readjust to the earth plane. When I was finally able to sit up and open my eyes, the room was immersed with moving patterns of light.

One of the most important goals that I sought to reach from my work with Almitra was to send a request out to the Universe, and to draw my soul mate into my life. I had been celibate for three years, not wishing to involve myself with anyone who did not vibrate with me on a spiritual level.

Incredibly, after thirty-six years of searching for true love and never finding it, my soul mate entered my life during the exact time I was sending out for him with the help of Almitra and her very special tabby stones. The immediacy of the answers to my heartfelt prayers was astounding. My loved one is with me now, a life-treasure, a gift from God. I feel very fortunate to have received this blessing, and I credit the crystal healings for the speed at which it occurred.

In retrospect, the joy and wonderment that I experienced from these healings is immeasurable, to say the least. I felt very loved and protected, and this feeling has remained with me to this day. I recall the night that I was reunited with my beloved sister, Almitra. She had told me later that the reason she had been staring at me that night was because I was surrounded by beings of light, and the energy radiating around me was hard to look away from.

Little did I know at the time the blessings that I would receive, and the paths that were opening up before me through my rejoining with Almitra, who is one of the kindest, gentlest, and most giving souls I have been fortunate enough to share my path with. Her healing and visionary abilities are very powerful, yet she remains down to earth and has a heart of gold. It is difficult to describe these very personal accounts of my experiences with crystal healing, let alone to condense them into a few paragraphs. I hope, dear readers, that you will all take the opportunity to experience this for yourselves, someday, whether in giving or receiving. We all have the capacity to be healers, and to be healed. God bless you.

### Korkee Cunningham

I live on a small island in the Pacific Northwest. The ferry run is approximately 10 minutes and my drive home is less than five. The pain in my chest began on the ferry and by the time I arrived home, breathing was such an excruciating

I live on a small island in the Pacific Northwest. The ferry run is approximately 10 minutes and my drive home is less than five. The pain in my chest began on the ferry and by the time I arrived home, breathing was such an excruciating process I assumed that not breathing would be the only cure.

"So this is how I die," I thought, with my husband yelling at me and me not able to get enough breath to yell back at him, let alone tell him I'm dying.

Well obviously, I didn't die, but I sure did hurt. I spent the night immobile, concentrating on my body and listening to the crackle of my lungs.

The next morning my sister informed me that I may have pleurisy. A name for the pain. I'm the type of person that wants to name the disease. My neighbor, a Christian Scientist, disagrees believing something about naming a disease is more or less renaming God. But for myself, a name helps me to locate the cure. I phoned a nurse to read to me from her medical book about pleurisy. I went to my children's nurse practitioner to have her listen to my lungs. The symptoms and the stethoscope confirmed pleurisy a "wait-and-you'll-get-better-someday" disease.

I don't like to wait, which is one reason I don't go to medical doctors. I knew Almitra had moved onto the Island and I had tried contacting her previously about teaching some gemstone healing classes on the island. Now I needed her for her skill.

Perhaps I should explain me. I'm a sorceress (though like most people I assume me to be normal and everyone else is just varying degrees of that normalcy.) So gemstone healing was not foreign to me, though I had never had the opportunity to be healed by one who knew the stones well enough to practice gem stone healing as a vocation.

I do not go to medical doctors at the first sign of a symptom. I am not opposed to the medical profession, I certainly trust my children's nurse practitioner. I am just not comfortable with the A.M.A. branch of health care.

I mention all this because I believe people need to realize that not every healer/doctor knows what they are doing or has the skill or gift to heal. A statement from Ann Landers comes to mind, "Out of a graduating class, there is always half that have graduated in the lower 50% of the class." As far as I'm concerned, Almitra graduated in the upper 50% and I don't really care where or how or what methods she learned her skill; she healed my pleurisy in one session and I could breathe without pain.

I have employed Almitra for two other "cures" where I felt gemstone therapy to be appropriate. Each time, the experience has been rewarding, insightful and healing.

Her use of grid and laser treatments have had the most profound effect on me as I can physically feel the movement and the departure of the disease. The laser treatment did leave me sore the next day, a lot like having had a deep Swedish massage. The grid felt intense at the time, but left no noticeable side effects the next day (other than feeling well, of course).

As with all serious disease, I feel a person should employ a professional, such as Almitra, to properly dispel the ailment. However, I also know that as individuals, we can get to know the power of the stones and in turn, heal and learn about ourselves. The next time you take vitamin C for a cold, try holding an amethyst, carnelian or some green tourmaline. It's not going to hurt you unless you smack yourself in the head, and what a lovely gift from the earth.

Blessed be.

### Ruth Richmond

My crystal healing with Almitra took place on the new moon. We were outside with a beautiful view of the water and the mountains. After asking me what I wanted, Almitra began with a prayer, asking for blessings and for my guides and her guides to help us with this work. She asked all

117

spirits not in harmony with the healing to simply leave and surrounded us with white light.

She put crystals on me and we started working together. She told me to breathe in pink light into my heart and let it flow out my feet. I thought I was doing that but she made a comment that indicated I wasn't. She got a huge crystal and put it above my head.

She later said there was a very dark man standing on my heart chakra, who had been trying to block my healing. Almitra said she had to call on one of her warrior spirit guides to get him away from me. (It was someone that I rarely spent time with.) I hadn't even realized I'd allowed him into my aura, or given him the power to be there. After that we were able to continue with the healing. We concentrated on opening up my heart and solar plexus chakras. Almitra had me do a lot of deep breathing, breathing in feelings such as peace, and also colors, and releasing feelings as I breathed out. I remember the crystals helping me to forgive my father and to let go of the anger, resentment, pain and hurt.

I also remember breathing in a lot of pink light and breathing in love for myself. Then Almitra had me breathe in images of what I wanted for myself.

I felt wonderful. A lot of people noticed a change in me. By the full moon, my life was totally different. A lot of old doors slammed shut, and new ones opened. I moved to a new apartment in a different town. I was relieved to be fired from a job I'd been very frustrated with. I abruptly stopped going to the spiritual group I'd been involved with for a few years and, after being solo for three years, there was a man in my life.

That crystal layout with Almitra was a very powerful and very positive catalyst for me. It's now a year later, and I'm a very different person, and I'm very happy with all the changes in my life and in me.

### Kathi Schlincover

When Almitra introduced crystals to me several years ago, my experiences were quite varied. I was told to attune myself to my inner self and to the vibratory rates of the crystals. When I felt a particularly harmonious vibration from a crystal, that one was mine. I was especially attracted to a "green" crystal off to the side, but didn't say anything, as it wasn't in the provided selection. When my son spotted it, and picked it up saying it was really special, it validated my feelings also. I held it against my chubby abdomen and felt a sensation of being cool, and my abdomen losing the fat, shrinking and flattening out. Almitra told me that the crystal was especially useful for abundance, and that same day, I found a "present" caught on a snag on the beach. My sense of prosperity has continued to increase since working with the green crystal.

Arthritis has plagued me off and on, and some intense experiences occurred when Almitra did healing treatments on me. She was guided to use all of her collection of laser wands on me, saying that my body just loves them. As she guided me through a relaxing meditation and began working on moving the energy out of the painful arthritic joints, I became aware of them as being like fire. She tuned into it psychically, and told me to visualize a cool, soothing green. When I couldn't do it, she gave me images of leaves on trees. I perceived them as being in their fall flame colors, and became somewhat frightened at my inability to work with that block. At that point, she sensed what I was experiencing, and later told me that was when she placed an emerald over my sixth chakra. That broke the block, and I was able to visualize the cooling green. The arthritis cooled down for awhile, but I needed further treatments.

My most profound experience with Almitra's healing treatments came when she worked on severe arthritis and tendonitis in my right wrist. As always, I relaxed into the

119

meditation and went to my particular spot in the woods to a great tree beside a path. She began using a laser wand on my wrist, drawing out the pain. All of a sudden, she jumped back and shook her hand off, asking me if I had felt that shock. I hadn't noticed any particular shock. She told me then that a great ball of pain energy had jumped out of my wrist into her hand, and she threw it away. From that point on, the pain was gone, and has not bothered me since. I love Almitra's lasers.

## Hal Booth
### Regarding a crystal healing session with Almitra:

The doctors had informed me that the angioplasty* that had been performed earlier had again closed up and that I had to reenter the hospital for another angioplasty.

I had one session with Almitra and could actually feel the "unclogging" occur, as well as a sense of rest and peace.

She did a series of manipulations/maneuvers with crystals and other materials (stone-types). She did some recitations of which I could not really decipher, had me see "blue, green and pink" visualizations mentally. I was amazed that I could see these colors as she instructed me to concentrate and visualize these penetrating colors.

I did again enter the hospital a short time later. They had me set up for an angiogram*, and then, an angioplasty. I informed them that I did not need an angioplasty, as I knew that the blockage was no longer there. Much to their amazement, when they did the angiogram, indeed there was no blockage and, therefore, I did not stay at the hospital but went on home.

I am looking forward to meeting with Almitra again upon her return to Washington state from Hawaii, and spend more time with her. This year has indeed been extremely busy, but I would like to have her do more "work" with me in the future.

* Angiogram is an x-ray procedure to see if there is a blockage present in the heart.
* Angioplasty is a surgical procedure used to remove heart blockages.

Chapter Eight

# Energy Clearings

All things store energy: cars, homes, offices and people.

*Without putting a judgment on the energy, either positive or negative, it is important to understand that energy is stored in everything. When one moves into a new home, the energies from whomever previously lived there will resonate until it is cleared. Whether or not we are conscious of what has occurred before we arrive, the energies will affect us.*

*When performing energy clearings, it is important to wear amethyst, as it will absorb all energies and recycle them back to light, protecting the individual from personally taking it on. I have been called on many times to assist in clearing energies in homes, cars and land areas. Removing the stored vibrations allows a fresh start to occur. While living on Kauai, I offered my services of energy clearing and balancing fairly often, as the culture presently there understands well the simple principle of energy clearing.*

*On one particular occasion my request for this service came through my higher guidance and, with the help of my spirit guides, I was able to follow through with the request and preform a clearing for a parcel of land that was sacred to the residents of Kauai. This parcel of land was known as Nukolii' before the construction of the Hilton Hotel, which now stands on this site. The residents of Kauai had voted to stop* construction, as they did not want anything built on this particular spot. My understanding is that this place is sacred ground to their ancestors (Hawaiian) because it overlooks an area where a battle occurred, and many warriors are buried nearby. Because the voice of the people was ignored and the hotel was built regardless, there was a deep, bitter resentment. It caused terrible disappointment and pain to many people, along with destroying their belief and trust in the local government. At one point, there was a bombing of the construction site and an on-going battle for many years. One can imagine the energies stored, both in the land area and in the hotel that was being built. I lived on Kauai during this period, and I can recall the anger people held within.

Towards the end of the construction period, plans were being made for the opening of the new Hilton Hotel. I had returned home from an afternoon at the beach and was in the shower getting the salt and sand off. Out of the blue, I was given this very clear direct message from my higher self: "You are to do an energy clearing and blessing of the Hilton Hotel and grounds before it opens. This is critical for all concerned." I immediately started talking out loud to my guides, while still in the shower. "Okay, you guys, but I'm not lifting a finger on this one. If you're serious, you'll have to set it all up."

And then I laughed to myself, "Yeah, right. I'm just going to walk into the manager's office with my sweet grass and crystals and tell him I need to clear and bless his hotel." I shrugged it all off and got out of the shower, wrapped up in a towel and went to the kitchen table to sit down. Well believe it or not, as I sat there, the next thing that came over the radio was an announcement about the new Hilton Hotel, naming the man who had been assigned as manager. I got a pen,

*wrote down his name, and laughed to myself as I thought,
"Okay, okay. You set it up and I'll do it. I've got to see this!"
The synchronicity that followed in coordinating the event to
follow was absolutely miraculous.*

*It was through a friend of mine who owns a jewelry store
that I was given the connection to meet with the manager of
the Hilton. I had told my friend, Charlie, that I had been given
the message to clear the Hotel. Charlie was familiar with my
work and his response was overwhelmingly in favor of the
idea. I left the introduction up to Charlie. He simply set up a
time for me to go to the Hilton and to meet with the manager
and then to do my work. At the time, I was working full-time
at a local jewelry store. I hadn't made any effort to arrange for
a certain day off or anything to set this particular event up. It
came as no surprise when I just happened to get a three-day
weekend off, starting the day before the Hilton was scheduled
to open. I was given the message via my friend as to what
time I was scheduled to meet the manager at the Hotel. I
arrived that morning, the day before the Hotel was to open,
with my sweet grass braid in one hand and my large bunch
of Hawaiian tea leaves in the other. In my pockets, I had an
ample supply of clear quartz crystals and a rose quartz.
Around my neck I wore a strand of amethyst crystals (I'm
sure I was an interesting sight to all I encountered). I found
my way to the manager's office and announced myself to his
personal secretary. I was then invited into his office. Much to
my surprise, I found him very open to the whole procedure.
He seemed to understand the need for the clearing and knew
what he could expect to receive once the work had been done.
I explained to him that I needed to start at the very top and
walk through the entire Hotel, and then I would go outside to*

work on the grounds. He said he would make arrangements to have a security guard meet me at the office and escort me through the Hotel. He told me that the very top of the building was still not complete and was off limits. However, I explained to him that it was very important to start at the very top and work my way down. He said he would get the keys to the unfinished area while I waited out front to meet the guard. Shortly afterwards, a young man arrived. I explained to him what I was about to do as we walked together down the hall. He stopped in the middle of the hall and told me that he had just been flown in from another hotel to help with that opening, and that he did not know the layout of the Hotel well enough to help me. He then told me to wait for him while he got me the correct person for this job, and he left just like that. I stood there patiently waiting for whomever was to come. About fifteen minutes later, an older Hawaiian man came up to me. His presence was comforting, and he asked me how he could help with the work I was about to do. I explained to him that I needed to start at the very top of the Hotel and literally walk through the entire building. He said that he had been a security guard from the very beginning and knew the Hotel very well. I followed him to the top of the building. I then stopped for a minute to say a prayer, and I lit my long sweet grass braid. I explained to him that at no time should he pass in front of me, but to just give me directions while following behind as to which way to go so I could be sure to walk through all of the buildings. He then told me that his great grandfather was a Kahuna, and that he wanted me to know that he understood what I was doing, and that he and many others were grateful for what I was doing. He only spoke to me one other time during the entire procedure, which was when we had come to an area on the first floor level with the ocean. He told me that this particular spot had given him much trouble. I asked him what kind of trouble, and he explained that it always had a peculiar feeling. He said he often heard loud noises (chanting) and had problems with the lights and other physical operations. I took a deep interest in what he was saying. I stopped for a moment to focus on white light, and I noticed that the wind had really picked up. I made a mental image of the area we were in and then continued on through the rooms of the Hotel. He then led me through a back door that brought us out into the kitchen. I was walking through the kitchen with the sweet grass smoking. I found out afterwards that the head chef had come running out to yell at whoever was smoking in his kitchen. Seeing me with my tea leaves and sweet grass, he stopped, instead, to watch me bless his kitchen. I later met the head chef one morning while I was having breakfast during a sales meeting. He recognized me from the day I had performed the clearing. He told me how he had come out to chase me from the kitchen because of the smoke and, of course, stopped once he saw who I was. He expressed his appreciation for my work and commented on the change in the energy once I had completed the clearing. Once I finished clearing the kitchen, I proceeded to the main lobby and then the bathrooms and store on the first level. Then I finished clearing the conference room, and from there he led me outside, where I began walking around the Hotel grounds. I circled completely around the grounds and headed down to the beach area. I stood there for a long time, trying to console the spirit energies that were present. I had a very difficult time convincing the present energies to give us their blessings. At one point, I didn't think I was going to be able to

receive their blessing as I watched the spirits leave. It was
something I shall never forget. As the spirit energies were
moving away from me, I got down on my hands and knees
and began digging a hole with my bare hands. There was a
dark cloud present and I could feel the anger in the air. This
was a very heavy, serious matter. I continued digging a hole,
and then I reached into my pockets and took out the crystals
I had brought. I held them up to the heavens and I said out
loud, "Please forgive those that have offended you. Their
ignorance has suffered them greatly. Please let it be forgiven
so that the beauty of this place and the creation now here can
be enjoyed by all peoples." I then placed the crystals in the
ground and buried them with the sand. I turned to face the
ocean and then stood up. I stood there and continued to wait
for a sign. I watched the dark cloud pass by and began to
walk back towards my car. I took the last bit of sweet grass,
(only a tiny bit remained), and threw it into the air. As I
walked onward, it began to rain. I felt the tears of the
ancestors falling on my face, and I felt a great compassion.
The rain stopped as I walked, and then the sun came out.
I continued walking, and as I came around the side of the
building and looked across the way to the mountains, I saw a
very faint rainbow. I felt a peace come over my being. I knew
from the omens I had been given that my offering had been
received, and I felt a deep gratitude. I walked back to my car
and went home.

The next day I was completely exhausted and spent the
entire day sleeping. I realized that my guides had known
what they were doing when they had arranged for me to have
three days off in a row. I was amazed at how this whole event
had come together, and felt blessed to be a part of the energy

clearing. I never received any formal thank you from the management of the Hotel, but while I was doing the clearing, many of the local folks who worked for the Hotel came up to me and told me they were very grateful for what I was doing. I told them I was very happy to do so. Their appreciation and ability to express their feelings will always mean a great deal to me. As for myself, I am grateful to have had the opportunity to remove the anger and bless the land.

Performing an energy clearing for your home, office, or any other structure is a simple procedure. There are a few important things one should remember.

First, always start at the highest point of a structure. Secondly, have your path laid out to follow so that you can physically walk through all parts of the building. It is very critical to keep one door open throughout the energy clearing. Walk towards the open door, and most important, walk completely through the open door outside and away from the structure as you release the energy returning it back to the heavens. To release the energy, simply hold your hands up as you focus, giving white light to the heavens. I strongly recommend the person performing the clearing to either carry or wear amethyst. Sage, sweet grass, cedar or any combination of these can be used to preform the clearing.

Make sure you light the plant and get a good smoke going before you start your walk. Please make sure you have something below your smudge while burning it to catch the hot ashes. For energy clearings in Hawaii, I always use sea salt and tea leaves for the work. The sea salt is placed inside in all corners of the building, and I carry the tea leaves during the clearings. There have been several occasions when I have put sea salt around a person's home or on the borders of their *property. These procedures can be followed to clear any structures. Once a person clears their home or office, they will be amazed at the difference in the vibration and clarity that will come into their environment. For any person who is involved in the healing arts, clearing the healing room or office is a must.*

Chapter Nine

# A Guided Crystal Meditation

This meditation is a wonderful tool in assisting one in meeting and
working with their spirit guides.

*The best way to participate in this exercise is to record the
following guided meditation onto a tape recorder. Your
subconscious will respond best to your own voice. Talk slowly
in a calm, clear tone when you record this meditation. Once
you have completed the recording, you will need a single
crystal and a quiet comfortable place to sit.*

*For this meditation, hold your crystal in your left hand,
close your eyes, and take in a breath while focusing on
breathing in peace. Once you have done the breathing and
centered yourself, crystal in hand, you may begin.*

In your mind, go to a place that is very sacred to you;
somewhere outside. Sit down on the earth, and feel the earth
underneath you. Feel the wind gently touch your face.
Become one with the environment. Feel it and breathe it.
In your hand you are holding a clear quartz crystal. Feel it.
Get to know it, and see it in your mind. Now, as you
visualize yourself sitting on the earth on this special place,
suddenly in front of you your crystal is sitting on the ground.
Your crystal is growing larger and larger and larger before
your eyes. It is now very large and tall standing before you.
Ever so gently and slowly get up and gracefully walk towards
your crystal.  Walk around your crystal until a door is

presented to you. Look at the door and find the handle, create whatever handle you desire. Lovingly, reach out, turn the handle, and open the door into your crystal. Go in through the door and walk around inside of your crystal. Notice the colors inside the crystal and feel the texture on the crystal walls. As you walk around, notice the golden light coming into your crystal. See the white light coming into your crystal. See all the colors of the rainbow coming into your crystal. The colors are dancing around as you walk inside of the crystal.  As you continue walking around inside of your crystal, you find a chair. This is your own crystal chair made especially for you. Sit down in your chair and feel the chair embrace your being. It is ever so comfortable. Sit there in your chair and just experience the feeling of being inside of your crystal. Breathe in the peace. Breathe in the healing. Breathe in the light. Take a deep breath and just relax inside your crystal in your special chair, and just be at peace. Your attention is drawn now again to the door of the crystal. Ever so gently the door is opening and into your crystal walks your spirit guide, your friend and companion.

This being is now walking towards you with love and light. As your spirit guide approaches you, next to you is a chair, a crystal chair. Your spirit guide sits down in front of you. Look into the eyes of your spirit guide, your friend. There is compassion.  As you sit there with your spirit guide inside of your crystal, listen carefully to the message your guide has brought you today. Listen with your soul, listen with your heart, and listen with your mind. Take a breath and breathe in peace as you listen to this message from your spirit guide, your friend, your companion, a being that is always available just for you. Sit there with your spirit guide for a moment in the crystal chair inside the crystal and just enjoy being united with this special friend. Look again, deep into the eyes of your spirit guide. Connect and  become one with your friend. The message that has come today has been delivered, ever so gently, ever so gracefully. Your spirit friend is standing up and walking towards the door. Your guide reaches around and opens the door and gracefully walks out of your crystal. As you sit there, breathe in peace knowing that this friend will never leave you and is always available to you at any given moment. The door is closing behind your spirit guide and once again you are surrounded by the peace and tranquility of your crystal. For a moment, remember the message that has been given to you today, the connection with your special friend, and rest in this knowledge. Stand up now inside your crystal, and reach your hands up to heavens and feel the healing energy coming through the top of the crystal bathing your being. Walk around once more inside the crystal and find yourself at the door. Reach out ever so gently and touch the handle, turn it slowly, and open the door. Step out of your crystal and walk through the doorway. Feel the earth, once again, under your feet. Walk back to your special place, and once again, sit down on the earth. Feel the wind gently on your face, and feel the earth beneath you. Listen in the distance. Hear the birds sing as you take a deep breath. Turn your attention to your crystal still standing in front of you watch as it begins to get smaller and smaller, until once again your crystal will fit in your hand. Feel the crystal in your hand, become familiar with the shape and structure of the stone. Now hold the crystal in both of your hands and bring the crystal slowly up towards your face. Gently open your eyes and look at your crystal. Bring your attention back to the place you are now sitting. Rub your hands together while holding your crystal, and take in a deep breath. Breathe in peace and breathe out peace. Remember that with your crystal friend you can journey at any time to meet with your spirit guide.

Chapter Ten

# The Inside Story

*Every member of the mineral kingdom has its own specific
characteristics and abilities, unique unto themselves. Each gem plays
its part in God's creation, where everything has a purpose.*

*I would like to introduce you to my friends, the rocks, as
they have made themselves known to me. Each presents
itself in its own time, and each one tells a different story .
This information is something that has come to me slowly
over a lifetime. As a young child, my special friends were
the rocks. I would collect and keep them under my bed in
shoe boxes, each one a treasure to hold, more precious than
my store-bought toys. I have always carried rocks in my
pockets and my purses for as long as I can remember. Over
that period of time, I carefully learned to understand the rocks
and to listen to their stories. It was my first American Indian
teacher who gave me the understanding of the rock's ability to
speak. As I became aware of their level of being, I, too, was
able to hear their stories and become one with the  rocks. One
realizes that not everything speaks our language, but surely
we know that communication is not limited to the English
language.*

*It has taken man a long time to accept the fact that
dolphins can communicate, and now man has realized
through experience that all mammals can talk. The American
Indians and the Kahunas, who I have studied with, hold so*

much in common. They believe all creation is living and has reason to be respected. Through this belief, I was shown that rocks, too, are alive, that they are here for a reason, and have their stories to tell. It has been shown to me over and over that rocks have a purpose, and that during this particular time before mankind, they have much wisdom and strength to offer us. Each crystal and gem is a tool. It is simply in learning how to use them that their benefits are received.

This chapter is written to give one an understanding of the different aspects of the mineral kingdom and to take a look at each type of stone, thus to see them on their own level. The information I am sharing is given through my own personal experience with certain gemstones. The uses and properties of each gem are shared with you based on my work with each stone, the characteristics I have seen while working with that particular stone, the way a stone has come into my life, and the information it has given to me. This knowledge is shared with you as it has unfolded along my journey into the mineral kingdom. It has only been in the last few years that people have begun to recognize that rocks, much like herbs, have specific areas of healing that they focus on. There are stones which are specifically useful for certain aspects of healing, and others that are useful during meditation, etc. It is one thing to tell you that this rock does this, or this rock does that. I'm hoping to avoid repetition and give you a better understanding of how I arrived at what gems are useful for. It is interesting to know that all members of the mineral kingdom are crystalline in nature. As crystals, they each have their unique qualities, thus affecting all that surrounds them.

# Clear Quartz Crystals

*The first crystal that made its way into my life was a clear quartz. I learned so much from this rock. A clear quartz crystal is an excellent amplifier of energy. In simply carrying a crystal around with me, I have experienced an increase in energy level. It does this because it has the ability to increase and amplify energy. By working with my natural energy, it simply extends my aura and thus makes my energy field larger and harder to penetrate. Overall, the results are better health and more energy.*

*Clear quartz actually works to improve one's immune system. When you wear a clear quartz crystal directly over your thymus (located in the middle of the chest), it will improve the performance of this glandular organ which, in turn, improves the overall operation of your body. This crystal is known to improve one's health at all levels. I have experienced it to bring healing to individuals on a general basis.*

*I have spent hours in meditation with clear quartz with one main question in my mind: What is the main reason you are here, as you are the most abundant mineral on the planet, and why have you resurfaced at this particular time? Aside from your wonderful abilities and thousands of uses, there has to be a specific reason you are here. The answer given seemed so obvious that it slipped by me. Since my first introduction to clear quartz ten years ago, I have seen that we, the people of planet Earth, are in the midst of a major energy acceleration.*

*One starts out very slowly when clear quartz is in their presence. As we are able to tolerate more energy, the pattern* moves upward. The more I work with clear quartz crystals, the more I am able to be around them; thus the span of time and the size of crystals increases proportionally. It finally dawned on me that my tolerance level was increasing along with my rate of acceleration. Then, the answer from the clear quartz was understood. Man is in the midst of a major shift of energy, and the Earth is in the midst of a major acceleration. Clear quartz is here to help us prepare for this energy shift. Without this assistance our bodies would literally explode! One might say,"Oh, I get it. This is why all of a sudden there is this mass attraction to clear quartz, and why so much of it is available." I know that this purpose is why so many of us have been involved in getting crystals out to the general public.

I have experienced a major energy shift since I was first introduced to clear quartz. It came very gradually. I drink crystal water daily and find myself able to be around large amounts of crystals without getting overloaded. I can remember when I first went to Arkansas, I was able to stay in the warehouse with the larger clusters for a maximum of forty minutes. The exposure time grows as one's energy level accelerates. I remember talking to the monks when they first received the large crystal on Kauai. It was very difficult for them in the beginning to be around the crystal for long periods of time. I talked with them about their levels of energy and how the crystal would accelerate their rate of vibration. I instructed them to take it easy at first and not to overdo it. I remember talking with Ceyon Swami about this information, and he told me he was experiencing dizziness and nausea. I assured him that it was an adjustment time for his body and energy field, and that it would go away. I asked him to

135

*please get some silica in the homeopathic form. Silica is an herb known as horsetail grass. I have found it to be very helpful when one is first adjusting to the higher vibrations of clear quartz because our bodies are crystalline in structure and composed of some of the same minerals as the crystal's silica.*

*Clear quartz is made up of pure silica and oxygen. The chemical formula (SiO2) is 46.7 percent silicon and 53.3 percent oxygen. For this reason, I have experienced these crystals pulling the silica out of my body. This is especially true if I am around a lot of crystals, working with them or handling them often. Another way we deplete silica from our bodies is when we do healing work or channel from our higher selves. We simply use up silica. Therefore, it is very important if you are around a lot of crystals, use them for healing, or work in a store that sells them, that you add silica to your diet. It can be found at any natural food store. Signs of silica burnout are dizziness, memory loss, light headedness, and headaches. Some people experience depression and withdrawal. After I spoke with Ceyon, I learned that both he and the other monks at the temple were adjusting fine to the increase of energy coming from the Earthkeeper. It is something you experience for yourself. The larger the crystals, the more you feel the change. Simply carrying one clear quartz crystal with you at all times begins the process of attuning your energy field to a higher vibration frequency. This is essential during the energy shift that will occur on this planet.*

*I have been shown many other uses for clear quartz crystals over the years. Knowing more about their purpose enhances my respect for them.*

*I have found they are not limited to one's belief in them. If I gave a crystal to someone who didn't believe it would still increase their energy and aura. Non-belief has no effect on the crystal's ability to work.*

*One of my favorite things to do with clear quartz crystals is to program them to help with a specific project or need I have. This is easy and they do a great job because of their natural ability to amplify energy. Our focus and intention transfer our thoughts into the crystals where our program is then amplified.*

*To program a clear quartz I always clear the crystal first. This is done with sage or cedar smoke. I have found this to be the simplest and fastest way to completely erase all other vibrations from the crystal. Just light the herb and get it to smoke, then pass the crystal through the smoke, ridding the stone of all energies and leaving it clear for the new program. I then usually take a few deep breaths and focus in my third eye what I want to manifest or accomplish. While strongly focusing on this thought, I blow into the crystal. I then write on a piece of paper what I am working on, date and sign it, and place it under the crystal I wish to program. This method has given me excellent results. For instance, I use it to program clear quartz crystals to purify water. Then I place them into my drinking water container. I have had great results using them in various water supplies. I have seen bad tastes and odors removed overnight. I have placed them directly into wells where water test results have documented improvements. Clear quartz has uses too numerous to list. One needs to simply get to know their crystals and spend time with them. More and more information is given as you listen directly from the stones.*

*The first clear quartz crystal I was given opened the door for me to understand how I could incorporate crystals into my healing work. Since this first clear quartz appeared in my life, I have been able to utilize their extraordinary gifts, open myself to their level of understanding, and improve my healing work many times over. Because clear quartz has the ability to store energy, one can work with them in such a way to pull out pain and to promote healing. I work very closely with clear quartz in the healing sessions I do. I can program the clear quartz tools I work with to remove pain and to restore healing. This simply amplifies my intention and helps to carry through the healing process. I have also worked with crystal grids, where I place a person within a pattern of clear quartz crystals. There are many different grids one can work with. I first began working with crystal patterns on myself after I had an injury to my left leg. I kept seeing this pattern of crystal formation in my third eye so I started playing around with crystals placed in circles. This led to different formations. I would lay out crystals in specific designs, and then sit inside of the grid. I began experimenting with double terminated crystal grids, which were fabulous. This information came through to me spontaneously. I remember feeling like there was more to the puzzle, and that I was definitely on to something very extraordinary. Approximately eight months later I received a copy of Frank Alpers book, <u>Exploring Atlantis, Volume I</u>.*

*After reading this interesting book, it helped me to fit all the pieces together. Frank is a person who channels information and is known to work with crystals in healing. This first book was very important to me. I continued to work with the patterns I had seen in my mind, along with the information*

*Frank had written. The puzzle was finally completed for me.
I called Frank one evening from Kauai and thanked him for
the information he had brought through. I know my soul has
experienced Altantis and Lemuria, and that a lot of the
information I bring through is from this period in time.
I hadn't set out consciously to channel anything. However,
this experience confirmed that this information is Universal
and available to anyone interested in learning it. I had
experienced this while on Kauai when Frank was thousands
of miles away somewhere in Arizona. We are both part of that
same experience. Frank was able to help me understand grid
patterns and how to access the information I was receiving
through his ability to channel information. I have continued to
work extensively with patterns and formations of crystals
around individuals in healing sessions and the results have
been tremendous.*

*One must also consider that within the quartz family, there
are a lot of variables. This adds to the unique qualities of the
crystals. Each specific type of crystal has its own particular
specialty. One finds in the clear quartz crystal collection a
wide range of different types of crystals. A few of the common
ones are: double-terminated, self- healed, rainbow quartz,
tabular crystals, and crystal clusters. Katrina Raphaell did
an excellent job of giving us a way to identify individual
crystal differences. She has classified crystals according to
their unique physical structures and individual uses. Katrina
was instrumental in giving us a way to communicate the
abilities of certain crystals such as the laser wands, the
record keepers, the channelers, and transmitters. In her books
she gives us an understanding of each kind of crystal and its
uses. Each one of these particular types of clear quartz has*

something unique that sets it apart. A clear, double-terminated quartz crystal carries all the qualities of a clear quartz, but along with these qualities, it has added abilities a person can benefit from, if one knows how to work with them. Because the crystal is terminated at both ends, it has the ability to send and receive information in both directions. I have found these doubles very valuable in healing. I place them in between the chakras that are blocked to restore a flow of energy between them. They are great to wear in the center of the body, as they help to balance a person in both directions. They help immensely with energy flows in the system, and for that reason, a lot of people are attracted to them. I love to use them in layouts, as they move energy so well in all directions when placed in a formation around someone.

A clear quartz with rainbows inside brings additional qualities. Each time I have shown these special rocks to people, there is a change on their faces. Some look at first in disbelief, then all of a sudden, once they see the rainbow for themselves, bingo! Everything changes! Their auras become lighter, and they always smile. It's a miracle! These wonderful creations bring joy to the individuals they meet. In healing work, the rainbow crystals transform a person who has suffered from trauma or shock. I have worked very closely with the rainbow quartz to remove buried sorrows in a person's heart chakra, and restored joy in place of their pain. I can remember a friend of mine on Kauai who lost her new puppy. She was heartbroken. I gave her a beautiful rainbow crystal, and it was amazing how it was able to comfort her. She came back to me a few days later and told me how that particular stone had helped her in her time of sadness. It had helped her to focus on the joy the puppy had given her instead of her loss.

My first introduction to tabular crystals was in Arkansas. Having access to literally thousands of crystals while I was there, I was able to see a lot of clear quartz crystals which were unique and somewhat rare. Up until this time I hadn't seen or heard of a tabular crystal.

My friend, Greg, who I spend a great deal of time with, truly turned me on to some of the most extraordinary crystals I have ever seen. He gave me my first tabular crystal. I call them "tabbies". Tabbies are really different from regular crystals, because they are flat. They still have six facets, but unlike the crystals one is used to seeing, they grow flat.

Greg explained to me that when the silica was flowing, the tabbies were formed flat because there wasn't room for them to grow in any direction except out. One can see they are very different by holding them in their hand. They look like something sat on them. They are completely flat and feel different.

I have become very fond of tabbies. I have spent a great deal of time working with them and have gotten to know and understand their special gifts. Tabbies are great tools for communication. I have used them successfully to connect with people who were not available via ordinary means of communication. For example, once I wanted to talk to a close friend of mine but didn't have a phone number for this person, and her whereabouts were vague. I simply programmed the tabby to have her call me and held the crystal in my right hand to send out this information. This is one of the areas these crystals excel in. It always works for me. Within a few minutes, the phone rang. I answered, "Hello, Patty. I knew it

141

*was you." I started to laugh and told her I now had a foolproof way to get in touch with her. I then told her about the tabular crystals.*

*A friend of mine came out to visit earlier this week. It was about six months ago I had loaned her a pair of tabular crystals to work with. She used the crystals to help her find her soul mate. I gave them to her and instructed her to program them to bring her life partner to her. She had been consciously working on herself in preparation for this person to come. (I know that tabbies, because of their unique ability to communicate on different levels, are the perfect answer for a person who is sincere about finding their partner.) She took a little bag out of her purse and placed these two tabbies on the table. She said she wanted to return them because she had definitely found her soul mate. She then thanked me for the use of them. I expressed my happiness for her and thanked her for returning my tabby friends. I was glad to see them again.*

*I have also worked directly with the tabular crystal to do lightwork at a distance. They are an excellent tool for sending information or healing to any person or place, anywhere. I work with them when I am doing a healing meditation for the Earth. When I want to assist an area that has experienced physical catastrophe, for example a forest fire, I will hold the tabby in my right hand and program the crystal to put out the fire. I then focus the crystal on the particular area, and I consciously send the program to put out the fire through the crystal. I have used this technique in various situations over the years. I am very sensitive to the Earth, and when there is a situation I am aware of, I know that I can go there with the use of these crystals and be a part of the solution. I learned*

this technique in my huna classes, and combined it with the
use of the tabular crystals to focus and amplify my abilities.
I have seen positive results with both individuals and earth
situations. I have also participated with collective consciousness during times such as the harmonic conversion. There
have been times set aside to focus on peace and healing the
planet, and I like to use my crystals with meditations to
amplify the energy. With the understanding that we are one
with all living things, a person can be a part of the solution.
I used to be overwhelmed with a lot of the problems on the
planet. Once I realized that I could become one with the
energy and send it my light and healing energy, I found more
inner peace. Now, where there is a crisis, I use my crystals
and do what I can to help from a distance. I'm currently
spending time sending energy to the Amazon Rain Forest. I
have been focusing on the problems in Africa and visualizing
peace. I consciously send these areas my light and healing
energies. I find no peace in worrying or in amplifying my
focus on the negative side. So I focus on the positive.

As a society, we are very affected by what we hear via the
news media. We tend to accept what we hear about the
weather and world situations as the way it has to be. If
mankind would, instead, be aware of what he takes on from
this source of mass programming, he could become better at
influencing things in a positive direction. When we realize that
our thoughts create, we will then become aware. This will
make us more sensitive, selective and conscious about what
goes on in our minds. Currently on the news, they are
predicting a major recession. It looks pretty grim. Think for a
moment. If every person who heard this forecast visualized
the economy getting better and focused his mind on a solution

instead of fearing the worst, I'm sure we'd never see a recession. Mankind is very sensitive and vulnerable to what they hear. Subconsciously, we accept it as the way it's going to be. We have to stop and think about what we want to co-create each time we hear a statement of prediction. In the last few years, there have been groups uniting their thoughts on positive outcomes. Many groups have focused on peace. I know, as sure as I am sitting here, this focus has made a difference. We have made so many incredible leaps worldwide in the past few years; it brings me so much joy. Sure, we have a long way to go, but let us not forget to acknowledge the progress we have already made. I think about the Berlin Wall coming down, the talks between the U.S. and Russia. It gives me hope. I envision the day when we will take apart all nuclear weapons and build an art structure entitled "Peace of Mind". I know there are others who have similar thoughts. Let us continue to work together and remember to make use of the wonderful tools from the mineral kingdom.

## Rose Quartz Crystals

This is the stone of compassion, straight from the heart of the creator. Among all of the wonderful crystals in the mineral kingdom, I have seen rose quartz give so much. Once one gets to know this lovely pink rock, they cannot help but feel appreciation.

Rose quartz is a stone I have been aware of for many years. Once I began doing healing work with stones, I saw what a gift the pink crystal was. I have experienced it as a great first aid for heartaches and stress. I got into the habit

*of carrying a large, smoothly polished rose quartz in my
pocket on a day I felt stressed out, or on a day I anticipated
high stress. Working so much with the public, I was always
taking the rose quartz stone out and letting people hold it. I
was amazed at how the stone always heated up in a person's
hand. I kept sharing with folks my rose quartz, telling them it
was a wonderful tool for bringing calm, peaceful energies.
The more I carried it around, the more I listened. I learned
more about this wonderful healing tool. It was through my
work on Kauai doing healing sessions when I encountered
women who had experienced great trauma to their heart
centers. I had been working with a woman who had gone
through a separation. Her husband had left her for her best
friend, and she was devastated. She came into the office
and I could literally see the hole through her heart chakra.
She was in terrible anguish. I talked with her and told her to
please get some rose quartz. She told me she was completely
broke and in despair. I then gave her a strand of rose quartz
and told her to wear it continually. I promised her that within
forty-eight hours she would feel better. I gave her my home
phone number and told her to call and let me know how she
was doing. Well, she called me two days later and told me
she couldn't believe the difference. She had definitely
experienced an improvement. She told me she was able to
set up a distance between her and her husband and begin
the process of standing on her own. I saw her shortly after
the call, and I must say, it was really amazing to see that her
energy had made a shift from one of terror and panic to one of
peace and tranquility. As I continued to work with this lady,
we made flower remedies and talked about the future. She
slowly got in touch with her feelings and made plans for her*

145

*life. She went through massage school and started her own practice. Her heart was healed and the pain removed. We saw it all change with the rose quartz. This particular experience was the most incredible witness to me about the healing properties of rose quartz. I have continued to use rose quartz with women and heart stress.*

*I have always had excellent results using rose quartz to dissolve sleeping disorders in men, women and children of all ages. This information about rose quartz really came through during a long distance healing session with a woman. I had sent her some rose quartz to assist her while she was going through a divorce. She started out carrying around a polished rock, and then started wearing it. One day during a phone session, she told me, "Almitra, you've got to try sleeping with your rose quartz." She went on to tell me how she had held the stone I had sent her in her hand all night and how it had changed her sleeping patterns and her dreams. At her suggestion, I started experimenting with rose quartz rocks under my pillow.*

## Dioptase

*My first introduction to dioptase came from a friend of mine named Susan. Susan, who comes from New York, is a person I acquire stones from. On the floor before me there lay an incredible array of gemstones, but immediately my attention was drawn to this fabulous, brilliant green stone. It was nothing like I had ever seen before. Yet somewhere, faintly in my memory, it spoke out to me. As I reached over to pick it up, I realized it was something I was in need of, and like a piece of a puzzle, we were finally united. As I sat there*

*holding this incredibly beautiful stone I felt an immediate
peace in my being. I realized that this stone was very special.
I immediately looked up at Susan and asked, "What is this?"
She said, "That's dioptase. That stone is for starseeds,
lightbeings and walk-ins." Bingo! I knew immediately why
I was drawn to this stone. Dioptase has become a very dear
friend of mine. I have used it religiously since that first
introduction; needless to say, I purchased my first Dioptase
from Susan. I found this stone to be very unique. It has the
ability to go within a person and transform the person from
the inside out. It does this with the most powerful form of
personal love I have ever experienced. This stone is an
excellent grounder, and surpasses any I have used so far.
It has the ability to ground one's energy on an intergalactic
level. For a lightbeing who has the ability to work outside
this dimension, this stone is definitely a must.*

*A few years later while traveling inter-island doing some
workshops, I met a woman who made gem elixirs. I gave her
my dioptase stone to make an elixir from it. She had never
seen or heard of it before and experienced a very powerful
connection with my precious friend. It was through this
woman that the gem elixirs came into my life. Being able to
take dioptase internally was a wonderful experience. I have
found it to help me ground my energies, and to integrate them
into a form I can present easily to others. This stone has been
a valuable tool in my life and in the lives of others that, like
myself, have felt out of place on this planet. It seems there
are a lot of folks who don't feel at one with what's going on
here. I have seen this stone, in particular, help people
embrace this feeling and be able to adapt to a certain level of
reality. There are numerous people on the planet who are*

*different and have felt rejected or have been treated as oddballs. It is through our ability to find the medium of love within ourselves that allows us to face the challenges of this world. It's important to realize that anyone who has expressed any extraordinary abilities has had a struggle in offering their gifts. Dioptase is a stone which helps people who face this challenge in their lives. The light and love that come through this stone are very powerful.*

*I have shared this stone with many people, and there is always a handful of people drawn to dioptase, head-over-heels. These folks fall into a group of individuals who, like myself, incorporate this lovely green stone into their lives.*

## Clear Quartz with Green Chlorite

*My first introduction to the clear quartz with green chlorite inside came through a crystal I received named Ru. These particular crystals are clear quartz. However, on the inside, there is a presence of green mineral chlorite. They are found in abundance in South America, and occasionally in Arkansas.*

*Remembering that all power comes from within, these crystals are simply tools that, when combined with your focus and intention, will assist you in manifesting what you ask for.*

*Ru came into my life with a family of green crystals from South America. My friend, Susan, had brought to the office a large assortment of crystals for me to select from. There they would be placed in the store for sale to the public. I picked up Ru, and that was the beginning for me. The introduction was given as follows: These crystals are focused to manifest, particularly in bringing large amounts of money. She then told* me that the one I was holding had a name, Ru. Well it is one thing to have someone tell you that a rock is capable of helping you experience abundance, and it is another to experience it firsthand. Abundance means different things to different people. My experiences with Ru proved to show me how to manifest in general. Working directly with Ru has been an extraordinary experience for me. I have learned how to effectively program and access the abilities of this unique kind of crystal. The combination of the green chlorite in the clear quartz gives these crystals remarkable abilities, and works to enhance their focus for manifesting. From that first day on, Ru had become a constant companion of mine. I took this crystal everywhere. I got used to holding it in my right hand, and learned a system of pulsing it with what I needed at any given moment. Working with this crystal was a crash course for me. I used it continually and, the more I worked with it, the more I learned about its abilities. The time I spent working directly with Ru was instrumental in developing the techniques for these crystals, and had a direct impact on my success rate. For me, abundance is one thing, but ease of operation is of vital importance for the overall picture. If I am in a situation where the traffic is jammed and I need to be somewhere, I simply hold Ru in my right hand, focus my attention on a clear path before me, and then pulse the need into the crystal. I have found that squeezing the crystal and pulsing it gives it a super charge, and almost immediately the results are there. I have used this particular technique over and over again with amazing results. I never program for anything not in my best interest, and always work within what I believe is possible. Creating a parking place in a crowded area where no empty spaces exist is an easy task *when working with these crystals. I have found that I can pulse one need after another into my crystal with excellent results. I have shared Ru with lots of people. I simply show them how to pulse the crystal for what they wish to manifest, and turn them loose with the crystal. Ru has become a dear friend to me. I have learned so many wonderful things while working with this crystal. Ru has also given me the hardest challenge I have yet to experience while working with crystals. Ru had expressed to me the desire to be returned to the ocean, wishing to assist me from there. This message stirred up a lot of feelings within me. I had become very attached to Ru and couldn't bear the thought of letting Ru go. I spent many months working to come to peace with the request I had received from my crystal friend. I worked with Ru in manifesting a trip back to Kauai, and I promised to place Ru in the ocean once we have completed a project we are working on. I was able to give Ru to a friend of mine with the understanding that once this certain project is completed, Ru would be placed in the ocean. I never thought I could give up Ru, but much to my amazement, Ru works with me just as well from a distance as when I could hold Ru in my hand. I realize that Ru has given me an important message in working through my attachment. I know that the important thing to remember is that crystals, too, are live energies, and they also have requests. Ru had given me much over the years, so I was able to feel good about honoring Ru's request to return to the ocean. I'll admit that the first few weeks Ru wasn't available to hold were definitely not easy for me. But once I remember where Ru is, and I recall the purpose Ru was programmed to fulfill, I can only feel good. Ultimately, I was able to completely release my attachment. I now understand* that, in reality, I haven't lost Ru-my crystal friend is still with me.

I can't stress strongly enough what powerful tools these particular crystals are. Over the years, I have had the pleasure to distribute many of these green wonders to others. I express to each person that the bottom line is understanding that they work with our focus and intention, and working with them allows us to create all we desire. Some people listen and respond with a bit of reserve, but given two weeks with a green crystal, the reports I receive from them are always the same-pure amazement. These crystals change one's situation and even the most conservative soul is convinced of their ability to manifest.

I have had numerous needs met while working with these crystals-anything from finding a lost friend at an airport, to creating a large sum of money within a particular time frame. There is one experience that definitely takes the cake. One Sunday afternoon, I left my island home and headed for Mt. Vernon which is an hour and a half trip, one way. I have a crystal display at the local food co-op, and was bringing in new merchandise to add to my showcase. I was under the impression that the store was open until six o'clock p.m. Much to my disappointment, when I arrived I found the store completely dark and locked. On the door were displayed the hours for Sunday and stating that it closed at four o'clock. I went back to my car and sat there, thinking to myself, "I've come all this way for nothing, and I have no idea when I can possibly make this trip again." Then I decided to ask my crystal, Ru, for help. If there was any possible way to get into the store, it would be with Ru's help. So I sat there in the car, closed my eyes and focused, "Okay, Ru, get me into the

151

store." I knew it was a long shot, but what the heck!

After a moment of focusing, I opened my eyes, and from my car I could see a man walk out the back door of a deli which is connected to the main store. He walked across the parking lot to dump the garbage. I quickly got out of my car, walked up to this man, and introduced myself as the person who has the gem display. I explained to him that I had come a long way to put new merchandise in the store. I proceeded to ask him if there was some way I could get into the store. He looked up at me and said, "Come with me. I'll have to ask Ru. She's in charge." I said, "Excuse me, did you say Ru?" "Yes," he said. "She's the cook." I stood there with my mouth hanging open as he took me to see Ru, the cook. I just stared at her for a moment, then I asked her if it was possible for me to put some merchandise in the case in the main part of the store. She said, "Absolutely. I've got to clean up for a couple of hours, so help yourself." I thanked her sincerely. She had no idea what had just occurred. I went back to my car to get my things and proceeded to fill the showcase. Ru later came over and we spent a long time connecting. It turned out that we had both lived in the same commune at different times. We were able to share a lot of valuable information about the whole experience. Toward the end of the conversation, I told Ru about my experience earlier in the day, how I was locked out and had a crystal named Ru. I explained a little about how the green crystals work and told her that my mind had been blown when the guy told me that he had to ask Ru if it was okay to come in after hours. We both had a good laugh, but this particular experience working with my crystal friend, Ru, stands out in my mind as very extraordinary. Once again, Ru had helped me to manifest my needs and allowed me to pass through closed doors.

I highly recommend these clear quartz crystals with green chlorite to anyone who has a goal or need they wish to create in their lives. Remember that when working with them, they simply amplify your focus and intention. They are tools, and in the hands of a person who has a sincere desire to make things happen, they will be a welcomed addition.

## Black Crystals

The day I received my first cluster of black quartz stands out very clearly in my mind. A friend from California had told me about these particular crystals and sent me one in the mail. At the time it arrived, I was at the office in Kapaa where I did my healing work. Once the box was opened and I removed the crystal, I knew immediately why it had come and what it was going to help me with. With the crystal in hand, I went directly to the beach and washed the crystal in saltwater. I was very excited about the stone that had just arrived. The communication between myself and this particular crystal was immediate. I knew exactly why and what to do with it. I had never seen a crystal like this before or ever heard of them. This particular crystal lost no time in demonstrating its abilities to me. I returned with the crystal to the office, and the second I walked back inside, things began to change. At that particular time in my life, I was at a crossroads and several different areas of my business and financial affairs were stuck. My partner and I were in the middle of some major changes and several obstacles were giving us a hard time. Within minutes, things started to change. We had people appear from out of nowhere bringing us items we needed. The problems we were having with our rental situation were resolved within the hour, and everything that had been a problem up until the crystal arrived was taken care of effortlessly. I felt the conflict I had with a certain person move away from us, and in general, felt as if a wall of powerful protection had been placed around us. I ended up taking this cluster with me to the store and felt the same thing happen there. All of a sudden, all negative energy simply moved away. This first introduction to the black crystals was very dramatic and powerful for me. This particular crystal made a definite impression on me, and helped me to understand the balance between dark and light energy.

I would like to explain how these black crystals come into being. Naturally these crystals occur as smokey quartz; however, they are not quite the same. In the earth they occur in the ground where a small amount of uranium exists near the crystals when they are formed. Naturally they are found in Utah but do not have the beauty and luster that is found with the black crystals. To explain further, the black crystals I am referring to have been exposed to a mild form of radiation, the same process that is used to sterilize medical equipment. What occurs during the mild radiation process is that the minute amount of aluminium that is naturally occurring in the clear quartz crystals is burned out and the crystals turn solid black. This process is actually a form of removing impurities in the crystals. I have worked closely with these crystals over the years, and I have grown to respect them. The process of being exposed to the radiation sterilization process somehow fine-tunes and amplifies their abilities to act as a shield. They are excellent at reflecting any negative energies, conflict, danger, or harm for the person who possess them. On occasion, individuals who don't quite understand the process are turned off to them. Once a person has an opportunity to spend time with them, they understand that in the process the crystals are perfected completely free from any impurities and reflect this back for us to experience. I have sent these crystals to many individuals. People place them in their cars and offices, and find that they bring immediate results. I have given these crystals to folks to take to court, and always, things change in the person's favor. They are great tools for anyone who works in any area of law enforcement or counseling, as they are powerful protectors and keep the negative forces away.

## REFERENCE FOR PROPERTIES OF GEMSTONES

**Adventurine**-cleansing for the emotional, mental, and etheric bodies; increases emotional tranquility, and inspires a more positive attitude towards life; physical healing for the heart; good for children with emotional stress.

**Amazonite**-soothing to the nervous system, much like turquoise--again, the color therapy principle comes through; a light stone that feels good to the wearer, and brings through peaceful energies.

**Amber**-has a direct link with the balance of the earth and all organic matter; acts as a harmonizer of yin-yang principles--male/female; brings through golden light; electromagnetic energies, etheric body, endocrine systems, spleen, and base spine are greatly benefited with amber.

**Amethyst**-protection in travel; keeps negative energy away from the wearer; a powerful transmitter and purifier of energy from a lower to a higher spiritual level--in this way helps one to access their spiritual path; very healing stone, as it helps to purify on a physical as well as spiritual level; excellent for asthma and any lung disorders; helps to balance misuse of alcohol and drugs; helpful with headache pain.

**Apache Tears**-both directly and indirectly transforms negative energies within the individual, bringing them to light; a stone of compassion and protection.

**Aquamarine**-allows one to absorb the vibration of the ocean; calming; brings one into harmony with themselves; clarity; self-confidence; peace--think of the feeling one receives while looking at turquoise ocean water--flowing and calming energies toward one's self; helps self-expression; strengthens the liver, spleen, thyroid, and kidneys.

**Azurite**-used primarily by healers; very effective in removing old emotional blocks; excellent for rebirthing; increases oxygen to blood stream; helps break down old patterns; enhances the meditative states; awakens the third eye; will draw out any physical or emotional impurities; healing for bone problems and arthritis; a consciousness expander; stimulates psychic abilities; amplifies a healer's abilities. One needs to work very carefully with this stone as it is very powerful.

**Azurite-Malachite**-Again, we have a very powerful tool in the hands of the trained healer. Excellent for penetrating the emotional and physical bodies to remove blocks on both levels; excellent for cancer patients; brings negative thought patterns to the surface for release. In combination, these gems truly assist one another.

**Black Quartz**-(heat treated) naturally occurs as smokey quartz; use this stone to keep away negative energies and to resolve conflicts; can be used in legal disputes; good to place in your car, your home, at work, etc, as they keep you safe and act as a very powerful shield for any unwanted energies.

**Blue Lace Agate**-balancing for the throat chakra; peaceful energies.

**Carnelian**-balancing for the second chakra; brings focus to thought forms; healing for the reproductive organs and infertility.

**Chrysocolla (GEM SILICA)**-charges the auric field; helps eliminate personal fears and quilt; calms the being; relieves worry where one might otherwise experience digestive problems; healing for arthritis; a continuation of turquoise, only on a higher vibration.

**Chrysoprase**-This stone has reached a high level of development and is an excellent balancer for the physical, mental, and emotional bodies while on the physical plane. This is an apple-green variety of quartz that brings about mental clarity and awakens hidden talents; gives insight into personal problems.

**Citrine**-activates one's mental powers; clears thoughts; brings in the golden light vibrations; balances one's solar plexus; helps the individual to awaken their personal power; manifests abundance for those who are clear with their purposes and goals in life.

**Clear Quartz**-increases one's energy; all-around healing; calms and soothes the emotional being while creating a balance with the emotional and etheric bodies; activates visionary abilities; a catalyst for change.

**Clear Quartz Clusters**-used for recharging other crystals, jewelry, and stones; sets up a positive energy field in your home, or wherever they are placed.

**Clear Quartz With Green (Chlorite) Inside Them**-This stone is a very valuable tool in helping the individual to manifest abundance, and will bring to the individual what they focus on. When working with this stone, the individual needs to work with their visual abilities and focus on what it is they desire to manifest. Hold the crystal in the right hand and simply focus and pulse the crystal. These crystals are a powerful tool to work with. Again, they work with your focus and your intention because quartz self-amplifies. The green chlorite amplifies abundance. They are manifesters, particularly of money and financial resources.

**Diamond**-has reached the highest vibration of the mineral kingdom; pure white light energy; can facilitate transformation on all levels and will amplify desires and magnify intentions. One needs to be clear of desires, greed, etc. It is good to place with other stones, as it will increase their potential. Diamond is a master healer, simply because of the brilliance of its light and the ability it has to pass through all matter. It removes blocks to crown chakra, leaving one open to receive information from higher self. It acts as a general cleanser for subtle bodies.

**Dioptase**-a stone for light workers, starseeds, and walk-ins; brings a person into personal transformation through the power of love; increases energy; brings personal power through and into action; grounding on all levels and dimensions for people who feel out of place on the earth plane--helps them find a way to relate.

**Double-Terminated (Clear Quartz)**-great for sending and receiving information; increases energy as they bring energy through both directions; good to wear in the center of the body.

They will focus energy up and down. Enhances meditation; used in healing to break up blocks between two chakras.

**Earthkeepers (Clear Quartz)**-These are large quartz crystals that are approximately 700 lbs or larger in size. They have reappeared after a long time. They are here to help us understand our place in the universe, and to help bring about a reunification with the earth and the other planets. They hold valuable information directly linked to the earth and her balance. They protect the earth and come forth when she is in danger. They are powerful pieces and are in the process of positioning themselves in strategic power centers on the planet. They are master healers for anyone in their presence, and work with the individual to access universal information. They are a tool for communication between the earth and other planets. They set up a powerful energy field wherever they are placed, and are very selective in where they choose to be. Earthkeeper crystals are believed to be the ones that were previously misused in Atlantis, thus resulting in the destruction of the continent.

**Emerald**-This stone is a symbol for truth, divine order, prosperity, and goodness. Its value in healing lies in its transparent green color, healing for the eyes and the emotional being. It balances the heart and helps to stabilize the personality and astral bodies while increasing psychic abilities.

**Fluorite**-good for grounding and meditation; healing for the bones and teeth; enables one to ground excess energies and function at optimum levels; lets one handle great amounts of energy in the physical body.

**Garnet**-healing for the neck and lower back; helps with memory and grounding; good for the blood chemistry and flow of energy.

**Hematite**-The iron in this mineral has a strong effect on the blood and will help to restore balance to any blood disorders. Healing for kidneys; increases assimilation of iron; excellent for grounding.

**Herkimer Diamond**-This is a very high energy stone that will greatly assist one in their pursuit of out-of-body experiences. Will allow one to fully experience their dreams and will greatly assist one in their visual abilities; eases stress.

**Jade**-This is a universal stone that will give positive results to any person who wears it. It is best to wear this stone by itself, and not with other gems. A stone of balance and peaceful energies; removes any blocks that would prevent healing in the individual; calming for the emotional and physical bodies; peace.

**Jasper**-balancing for the second chakra; builds a strong immune system; increases a person's sensitivity picture; can be used for past life memory and soul recall; brings information from higher self into action. Astral and etheric bodies are balanced.

**Kunzite**-heals and soothes heartaches; opens the heart chakra to receptivity; a great love stone; balances and brings peace to the individual; use in relationships of higher love devotion; opens for spiritual love, compassion; removes fear.

**Lapis Lazuli**-increases wisdom; third eye awakener; protection; enhances self-discipline and mental clarity; increases psychic abilities; relieves anxiety and tension; opens throat chakra.

**Lepidolite**-This stone is an excellent stone to use for emotional imbalances. To use the stone in the raw form, simply rub the stone into the palms of the hands, thus receiving the natural lithium in the stone. Works great to relieve mood swings; reduces anger, hostility, and unreasonable fears. I have used it successfully to relieve bad headaches; I simply rub the raw stone on the areas of greatest pain. The polished stones are great to use in layouts to balance the third chakra and bring about emotional stability.

**Malachite**-aligns the etheric and emotional bodies; helps improve self- expression; useful for detoxification of the system; promotes right and left brain balance; relieves nervous tension; will enhance moods.

**Moonstone**-lovers' stone; helps one get in touch with astral and emotional bodies, intuition, and mystical side of life; a mood enhancer. As the moon changes cycles, people with severe mood swings need to respect the amplification qualities of this stone. Good for any female disorders; helps one get in touch with the goddess energy; feminine balancer.

**Obsidian**-protects the kind-hearted person; a protection stone; grounding; good for the first chakra; keeps negative forces away from the individual wearer.

**Onyx**-used to balance the first chakra; grounding; brings on objective thinking; removes negative thought processes; control over emotions and passions; balances male and female qualities; increases higher inspiration; strengthens nails, hair, eyes, heart, and kidneys; relieves neurological disorders, apathy, and relieves high stress.

**Opal**-This stone works with the law of return in relation to an individual's personal Karma, and is not the gem that brings forth action. This stone is worn successfully by individuals who are at peace with themselves. Because of the variety of color in opals, these gems have a broad range of healing abilities in relationship to their colors. Amplifies moods.

**Pearl**-helps us to be in touch with the ocean energies; excellent for the person who lives a high-stress life; calms and removes stress; good for arthritis and bone disorders.

**Peridot (Olivine)**-an all-around healing and regenerative stone; light energy; helps one on the path of light to shine their truth. This stone is found all over the beaches in Hawaii at night because it glows in the dark.

**Phantom Cyrstals**-very focused energy; pure light energy; very happy stones; the ability to connect the owner with the pyramid forces on this earth--those seen and unseen; great for use in meditation to connect one with their higher light-self, and for personal healing meditations; useful in sending light and higher love to any one or thing.

**Rhodochrosite**-heart chakra balancer; helps access higher self; soothing; calming; emotional balance; peace.

**Rhodonite**-develops a sense of self-worth and confidence; brings calm energy; alleviates anxiety, confusion, and mental stress; heart chakra healer.

**Rose Quartz**-removes stress; calming; increases peace for the heart chakra; heals inwardly; brings more love to the individual; Great for sleeping with--will allow a person who has trouble sleeping to sleep peacefully and undisturbed; used to help children who awaken a lot at night--place under pillow or mattress for small children; peaceful dreams.

**Ruby**-the stone of spiritual devotion, love for God, and the spiritual path; helps focus thoughts; will amplify thought processes. The user needs to have good control of their thoughts or this stone is in the wrong hands. High energy stone; works with individuals on a path of truth, divine love, and divine will; healing for heart chakra; Clears issues with father; circulation enhancer.

**Rutilated Quartz**-an excellent stone for healers; allows the healer to ground and remove unbalanced energies; a powerful healing stone; high energy stone; physical rejuvenation for our life force; balances electrical energies in the body; regeneration of the entire body; protection from radiation; eases depression. All chakras are aligned.

**Sapphire**-stimulates a desire for spiritual enlightenment, prayer, devotion, and a quest for inner peace; healing for the stomach and intestinal tracts; a link for the body, mind, and spirit towards self- clarity; an anti-depressant; amplifies thoughts and increases psychic abilities, clairvoyance, and telepathy.

**Smoky Quartz**-prominent for increasing self-esteem; keeps negative energies away for the wearer; good for removing unclear thought forms in meditation; awakens one to their kundalini energy; keeps the aura free of unwanted spirit energies.

**Sodalite**-similar energies to Lapis (not as strong); brings balance for glands emphasizing metabolism; inspires spiritual growth.

**Sugilite or (Luvulite)**-excellent for the third eye; awakens one's ability to see; a stone that is regenerative and healing for the healer; a spiritual stone that works with the person on a spiritual path; brings about unity with all life forms; helps one to communicate with their spirit quides and unseen helpers; excellent to improve meditation and access higher thought forms.

**Topaz**-calms the emotions, relieves tension and restores physical balance; protects against outside influences of stress; stimulates creative flow; increases energy; universal balance; works to bring deva kingdom into play.

**Tourmaline**-calms the nerves; a healing and regenerative stone; manifests wisdom; dispels fear and produces tranquility for the individual; a high energy stone; heals relationships.

**Tourmaline (Black)**-balancing for the first chakra. Imbalances with this chakra can include arthritis, dyslexia, heart diseases, and anxiety. It protects the wearer against negativity (particularly as it does not store negative energies) and removes them by deflection rather than by absorbing them. Therefore, this gem is first in line for those individuals whose job is to work with negativity, (police; counselors etc.) and for individuals who feel more vulnerable to negative energies. Good protection from the earth's radiation.

**Tourmalinated Quartz**-is where you find clear quartz crystal combined with tourmaline. This combination is very effective in eliminating any source of negativity. One needs to recognize that negative energy has its part in the evolution of the earth and, indeed, exists just as the light side does. One simply needs to learn how to effectively balance and confront these energies, and I have found these stones to be a very wonderful tool in doing just that.

**Turquoise**-a master healer; protects against environmental pollutants; increases psychic abilities; improves meditation, and increases peace of mind; a sacred stone to the American Indians.

163

**Zircon**-calms the emotions; helps with insomnia; brings about a more pleasant personality; balance for the liver; spiritual love; aligns the emotional, spiritual, and astral bodies; helps one to integrate visions and incorporate them into a form that is acceptable.

* * * * * * * *

*I offer this information as a guide based on my personal experience with gemstones. Please understand that it is not meant to be a final statement for any gem. I have limited this information to include only the gems I have had personal experience with. For this reason, there will be some gems I have not written about. If you seek additional information, it is best to consult the gems themselves, as they are our best teachers.*

# Glossary

**Affirmation:** A positive statement one can either write or repeat over and over. It is a thought focused with intense concentration, used to align the subconscious towards the realization of the goal. Example: "All that I need now comes to me easily and effortlessly."

**Atlantis:** An ancient civilization that was advanced as far as crystal uses were concerned. This area is now known as the Atlantic Ocean.

**Aura:** The energy field present in and around living beings. An extension of ones natural energy field, usually radiating between three to seven feet around the body and often seen in different colors or shapes around a person. Trees, animals, and other matter also have auras.

**Cellular Level:** On the level of an individual (singular) cell.

**Chakra:** An energy center found in the physical body. Man has seven major chakras: one at the base of the spine, one just above that, one at the center of the stomach, one at the heart, one at the throat, one at the third eye and one at the top on the head.

**Church:** A religious organization where the members believe and worship in a similar manner.

**Collective Consciousness:** Where a large group of people focus their thoughts or actions together consciously.

**Deva:** A being that is living in a higher astral plane. There are flower devas, rock devas, tree devas and water devas. Also known as angel, a light being.

**Eternity:** Without beginning or end; everlasting.

**Etheric Body:** That which exists beyond the physical body. That which is the subtle body or inner body.

**Flower Essences:** A tincture made entirely from the essence of flowers used for emotional healing. The essence is placed in pure water and taken internally.

**Gem Elixirs:** A tincture made by placing a gemstone in water, where it is allowed to transfer the gem's vibration into the water. This elixir is then taken internally by the individual for healing and spiritual growth. Each specific gem has its own focus for healing. This practice was utilized by ancient civilizations and has been used in countries such as China, India and Japan throughout time.

**Guru:** A spiritual teacher or master.

**Guru Purnima:** A ceremony held once a year on the full moon in July where all Hindus pay respect to their Guru.

**Gurudeva:** The shining spiritual being who is the destroyer of darkness or ignorance. An affectionate yet respectful term used to address the Guru or spiritual master. A name used for his holiness, Sivaya Subramuniaswami.

**Heau:** In the Hawaiian Islands, a Heau is a sacred site built often from rocks or many layers of rocks. An altar or a place where religious ceremonies and Hula dancing were preformed.

**Hindu:** A follower of Hinduism.

**Hinduism:** Known as the world's most ancient religion. The religion of the Vedas often known as the Sanatana Dharma or eternal faith.

**Huna:** The generic term for the knowledge of the Kahunas. That which is hidden, concealed, or not obvious. "The secret".

**Iraivan:** The all-pervasive one who is worshipped.

**Kahuna:** A priest, minister, sorcerer; an expert in any profession.

**Kalalau Valley:** A remote valley located at the most northern point on the Island of Kauai. This valley is only accessible by foot via an ancient trail that winds along the Napali coast line. Kalalau means healing light; the valley of the healing light.

**Kundalini:** The spiritual energy that is found to lay at the base of the spine. Through active yoga and meditation, the energy is awakened and rises up the chakra centers and onto the crown chakra. The Kudalini is also known as the "serpent power".

**Lemuria:** An ancient civilization that existed in the area now known as the Pacific Ocean.

**Meditate:** To quiet the mind and to go into another level of deep thought which often leads one to intuitive discovery. The art of focusing one's mind on a specific object or thought without interruption. A peaceful state.

**Puja:** A Hindu spiritual ritual or worship performed to call upon the deity and to establish a connection with the inner worlds.

**San Marga:** A spiritual sanctuary located on the Island of Kauai. Future home for the Iraivan Temple and Crystal Lingam.

**Siva Lingam:** Mark or symbol of God. The Siva Lingam is the simplest and most ancient symbol of God. (Siva) Lingams are usually stone, but may also be made of metal, precious gems, crystal, wood or any natural substance.

**Spirit Guides:** Light beings (souls) that exist in other dimensions. They come forth to an individual with the goal of service to that person.

**Stapathi:** A Hindu that is a temple designer and builder passed down through generations of families who are temple designers.

**Swayambhu:** Naturally formed, not touched, by man.

**Telepathy:** The exchange of thoughts between two people from any distance. This communication occurs without the traditional forms of thought exchange or normal senses being used.

**Soul:** An eternal and spiritual body of light.

**Swami:** Title for a holy man.

**Temple:** A spiritual sanctuary where one comes to worship God. A sacred place.

**Vision:** An image that appears to one in the form of pictures or impressions while the person is awake or in the state of meditation. Not an imaginary thought or dream.

**Vow:** A promise that an individual makes to their higher self (God).

**Wailua:** Name of the sacred river on Kauai that winds through the valley that is below the San Marga Sanctuary. The Hawaiian word meaning "spirit"or "ghost".

**Walk-Ins:** A highly-evolved spiritual being that transfers its soul into an adult body with prior permission from the previous occupant who has a desire to leave. Evolved beings who have come forth at this time on earth to help. Most walk-ins who come are peacemakers, healers and teachers.

*ORDER FORM*

## Armida Press
## Post Office Box 1210
## Kapaa, HI 96746
### Telephone Orders: 1-800-933-4991

_____ copies of **A Crystal Journey** @ $12.00 each

*Complete satisfacation is assured or please return any purchased book for a complete refund.*

Name: _____

Address: _____

City, State, Zip: _____

**Shipping:**    $1.00 for the first book and $.25 for each additional book.

_____ Please send my order air mail. Air mail charge $2.50.

**Personal checks, money orders, MasterCard and Visa accepted.**

**No CODs please.**

Total enclosed $_____

*Visa/MasterCard #* _____ *Exp.* _____

*Signature* _____ *Date* _____

Thoughts & Things

There is no time
like the present

Thoughts & Things

Walk in beauty,
peace and harmony

Thoughts & Things

Now is the
Moment of Power

Thoughts & Things

Love is
all there is

Thoughts & Things

First
things
First

Thoughts & Things

Forgiveness is
the key that
unlocks
all doors

Thoughts & Things

Grace

Thoughts & Things

*I will do what
I will to do!*

Thoughts & Things

Breathe in Peace

Thoughts & Things

Breathe out
Peace

Thoughts & Things

OM Namaha
Shivaya

Thoughts & Things

Aloha